AN ISLAND HELL: A SOVIET PRISON IN THE FAR NORTH

AN ISLAND HELL:

A SOVIET PRISON IN THE FAR NORTH

BY S. A. MALSAGOFF TRANS-LATED BY F. H. LYON

ISBN: 978-1-963956-60-3

Contents

AUTHOR'S NOTE

I and my four companions left the Solovetsky Islands (called in this narrative the "Solovky," the name by which they are commonly known) on May 18th, 1925, and crossed the frontier between Russia and Finland on June 15th. But it was not until eight days later that we reached Kuusamo and ascertained positively that we were in Finland, so that our journey lasted thirty-six days.

As I had supposed, I found that outside Soviet Russia the whole circumstances in which those transported to the Solovetsky Islands are compelled to live (or, it would be more correct to say, to die) — the whole life, regime, conditions of labour, food, and the other internal and external characteristics of the Solovky, were absolutely unknown.

The secrecy which enwraps the Solovky is quite comprehensible. The Soviet papers, concealing the grim truth from Russian readers, pass the Solovky by in complete silence. Foreign newspaper correspondents are not allowed to go there. There had not been, till we got away, a single case in which a prisoner had succeeded in escaping across the frontier, whereby the public opinion of Europe could have learnt the truth about the Solovky.

Providence thought fit to rescue me, by a miracle, from this place of torment. And I count it my most sacred duty to tell the world what I saw, heard and went through there.

These notes, of course, make no claim either to literary qualities and beauty of style or to exhaustive completeness. I look upon them as the testimony of a fair witness who speaks the truth and only the truth. And if my testimony is recognised as worthy of consideration, and is accepted as a part of that gigantic indictment which the Russian nation, the whole of humanity, history and God will without doubt bring forward against the Soviet power, I shall consider that my duty has been discharged.

In confirmation of my claim to have been, to the best of my power, impartial in my exposition of the facts, I may say that when I showed these notes to my comrades who escaped with me they were of opinion that, in my description of the regime in the Solovetsky Islands, I had in many cases been too moderate.

MAP OF THE CAUCASUS, TO ILLUSTRATE PART I.

PART I (Introductory) FROM BATOUM TO THE SOLOVETSKY ISLANDS

I. A WHITE GUARD IN THE CAUCASUS

Denikin's Failure — Guerilla Warfare — An Unexpected Blow — The Elusive Tchelokaeff — A Treaty that is Observed.

Before proceeding to my main task — an account of the conditions in the Soviet prisons in the Solovetsky Islands — I should like to dwell briefly on the period of my life which immediately preceded my transportation to that place. I think that this period is of more than merely personal interest. As far as I know, the punitive activities of the Soviet power in the Caucasus after the crushing of the armed anti-Bolshevist rebellion there have not found a place in any book of memoirs.

At the time of the final retreat of General Denikin's forces I was in the ranks of the Caucasian Army (on the Tsaritsin front). The disaster to the Volunteer Army compelled us all to take refuge in the mountains. Keeping touch all the time with the attacking enemy, our cavalry brigade reached the river Terek, where it was dissolved. The most reliable elements of it crossed the frontier of Georgia, at that time still an independent State.

In Georgia, the members of the brigade who were fit for service were incorporated by Keletch Sultan Hire in a cavalry regiment. Its duties were to execute raids on the Soviet rear and throw it into confusion, to destroy roads and excite rebellion against the Bolsheviks.

The raid into the Kuban planned in the summer of 1920 by the staff of General Wrangel, who was then in the Crimea with his army, gave Sultan Hire the idea of sending us also to the Kuban in the hope of inciting the Cossacks to rebellion. In the Kuban, we took part in the retirement of the invading troops to the Crimea, the raid having considerably outgrown its original dimensions. The bold plan of bringing about a rising did not succeed. We were dissolved once more.

In exceptionally difficult conditions, surrounded by troops of the Red Army, we formed a new detachment under the command of Colonel X (I cannot give the colonel's name; he is still carrying on guerilla warfare with the Soviet power in the Caucasus). Our detachment, despite its small numbers, waged warfare of a kind with success, and we were beginning to think of operations on a larger scale, when we unexpectedly lost the support on which we absolutely depended and counted; the famous "national rebellion" took place in Georgia. In reality the country was occupied, almost without resistance, by regular troops of the Red Army. Our detachment retired fighting through the wild mountains to Batoum. Here part of it was broken up and turned into larger or smaller bodies of insurgents, part left for Anatolia.

I made my way to Ajaristan. Thence communication was established with Trebizond, where Y lived; his name, too, I cannot give in full for the reason stated above. Until the autumn of 1922 we and Y organised frequent raids on the Soviet Russian frontier.

Then, as now, the unofficial direction of the whole insurgent movement in the Caucasus was in the hands of the well-known Colonel Tchelokaeff. Thanks to extensive help from the population, which sympathises with the "Whites," and to his own bravery and skill, the Bolsheviks have found Tchelokaeff quite uncatchable.

I know for a fact that the "Gruztcheka" (Georgian Tcheka) and "Zaktcheka" (Trans-Caucasian Tcheka)[1] have repeatedly attempted to buy him; they have repeatedly offered him huge sums in gold simply to leave the Caucasus. They even offered him a villa in any country in Europe he liked to name. The elusive colonel, however, rejected these proposals with disgust, and is still carrying out surprise attacks on one or another stronghold of the Soviet power in the Caucasus.

Between Tchelokaeff and the Communist authorities of the Caucasus a peculiar treaty exists. The colonel's family has for several years been confined in the Metekh[2] at Tiflis, a prison notorious for the cruelties practised there. The Bolsheviks, of course, would have shot them long ago, had not Tchelokaeff captured and hidden in a remote spot, as hostages, several of the most prominent representatives of the Soviet power.

When the colonel heard that his family had been arrested, he sent the following letter to the presidential body of the Georgian Tcheka:

"I shall send forty Communists' heads in a sack for each member of my family murdered by you. — Colonel Tchelokaeff."

So the Tchelokaeff family and the Communist hostages are still alive.

---

1   i.e., Gruzinskaya (Georgian) and Zakavkazkaya (Trans-Caucasian) Tcheka.
2   The former palace of the Georgian kings, used as a prison for many years past.

II. A FAMOUS "AMNESTY"

My Foolish Credulity — A Boy Tchekist — Taken Out to be Shot —
Mutual Reprisals — A Gallant Mountaineer — Identified by an Imbecile.

In November, 1922, in honour of the anniversary of the October Revolution in 1917, the Council of People's Commissaries of the R.S.F.S.R.[3]
(Russia then still lived under that pseudonym) extended a full amnesty
to all opponents of the Soviet power. This amnesty, which was signed by
the flower of the Communist Party, formally promised complete oblivion
of every manner of offence committed by White Guards of all ranks and
categories.

I cannot say how I, who knew better than anyone the value of Bolshevist promises, who had waged a life-and-death struggle with the
Soviet power for so many years, could have believed in the good faith
of people who always lie. I paid for my unpardonable stupidity by my
sufferings in the Solovetsky prison. May my fate serve as a warning to
other credulous people!

On April, 1923, I presented myself at the Tcheka offices at Batoum. I
was interrogated by an examining judge remarkable for his youth — an
impudent lad of seventeen. The detective service in Soviet Russia is brilliantly staffed! When he had totted up my "offences" in detail, the boy
Tchekist concluded his interrogation with the jeering cry:

"Ha, we don't use kid gloves with fellows like you!"

Nor did they. When I referred to the formal phrases of the amnesty,
the examining judge roared with laughter.

"Take him to the cells. They'll show him the amnesty there."

They did.

I will not describe in detail my moral and physical sufferings, the
blows, the insults, the attempts to extract information from me by provocateur methods, which I endured while in the custody of the Batoum
Tcheka. Suffice it to say that I was finally taken to be examined at two
o'clock in the morning. They again went through my biography for the

3   "Russian Socialist Federated Soviet Republic." The present official
designation of Soviet Russia is "Union of Socialist Soviet Republics"
(U.S.S.R.).

last few years with the greatest exactitude, and proposed that I should confess everything and name my principal accomplices, ten in number (the number was given quite correctly). Persuasion was exchanged for abuse, and abuse for revolver shots over my head to intimidate me.

I denied my guilt, and refused to name any accomplices. I and three other men were taken into the yard to be shot. They killed one prisoner two paces from me. The second likewise was shot dead. The third fell, covered with blood. They yelled at me:

"Now it's your turn!"

I stood beside the bodies of my companions in imprisonment. Almost touching my head with the muzzles of their revolvers, the Tchekists exclaimed:

"Now confess!"

I was silent. For some reason they did not kill me. Probably my life was still useful to them in some way.

I spent a few days in the prison of the Batoum Tcheka. Then they took me to the Trans-Caucasian Tcheka at Tiflis; its headquarters were in the Sololaki quarter, in the centre of the town. As regards cruelty, there was no difference between the regime there and that at Batoum. The president and omnipotent master of the Trans-Caucasian Tcheka was at that time the well-known Tchekist Mogilevsky,[4] who was killed not long ago in an aeroplane accident.

Blood was flowing in streams in the Caucasus. The Communists were taking a triple vengeance on their prisoners for the murder of Vorovsky in Switzerland, the insurrection in Georgia and Lord Curzon's ultimatum. In the countless prisons of the Caucasus thousands of people were being slaughtered daily.

The Caucasus has not yet been finally pacified by the Communists, and at the time of which I write the whole country was ablaze with civil war. Insurgent bands burst into the towns and hanged all the Bolsheviks. The latter replied by intensifying their already merciless reign of terror.

One day the rebels descended on the "Kursk settlement," close to

4   Mogilevsky was Mrs. Stan Harding's examining judge during her imprisonment in Moscow in 1920; see her book "The Underworld of State" (Allen & Unwin).

Vladikavkaz, and, among other things, drove off the herds belonging to the Soviet. A pursuit was set on foot, headed by the celebrated executioner, the Lett Shtybe, President of the Gpu[5] of the Mountain Republic. The rebel band went into hiding in the mountains, taking the cattle along with it, and could not be traced. The Tchekists succeeded in discovering and surrounding in the mountains only one rebel leader.

The mountaineer, with a precipitous wall of rock behind him and plenty of cartridges in his pocket, withstood an attack from several squadrons of Communists for several hours. One of his well-aimed shots killed Shtybe himself. Although several times wounded, he killed eleven more Communists. At last he fell mortally wounded. In his rifle, which his cold fingers held close to his face, not one cartridge was found; he had fought to the last. He was tied to a horse's tail and dragged to Vladikavkaz.

The executioner Shtybe was buried with pomp and ceremony in the Pushkin Square at Tiflis. The death of this rascal was made a pretext for reprisals against the prisoners.

The cowherd in charge of the beasts which the insurgents had driven off into the mountains was a boy, deaf and dumb from birth, and clearly half-witted. This imbecile creature was ordered by the Tchekists to identify, from among all the prisoners in the gaols of the Caucasus, "those concerned in the murder of that unforgettable champion of the happiness of the proletariat, Comrade Shtybe."

The presidential body of the "Gortcheka" (Tcheka of the Mountain Republic)[6] did not trouble to ask itself how we, who had been in a Tcheka prison at the time of Shtybe's death and long before it, could have been concerned in his "murder." We were drawn up in two ranks. If the cowherd stopped in front of a man, uttered an inarticulate sound, or simply smiled foolishly, it was considered sufficient proof that the man who had attracted the half-witted boy's attention had "murdered the unforgettable Comrade Shtybe." He immediately received the order, "Two paces to the front!" and a bullet was put through his head.

Several dozen men were killed in this manner before my eyes. Then,

---

5   Gpu (Gosudarstvennoe Polititcheskoe Upravlenie), the present official designation of the Tcheka. The sham "abolition" of the Tcheka in 1922 and its "replacement" by the Gpu are ironically described by Mr. George Popoff in his book "The Tcheka." The synonymous terms "Gpu" and "Tcheka" are used indifferently by the author.

6   In Russian Gorskaya Respublika, hence the portmanteau-words "Gortcheka" and "Gor-Gpu."

walking along the second rank, the cowherd stopped before me. Death seemed inevitable. But, apparently, the public prosecutor of the Mountain Republic, Toguzoff, who was walking behind the cowherd, and who had interrogated me only the night before and knew perfectly well that I had absolutely nothing to do with Shtybe's death, felt a momentary prick of conscience, and led the cowherd on just as he was distorting his countenance in an idiotic grimace before me.

This public prosecutor is a characteristic figure. Kazbek Toguzoff, an ex-officer, in 1917 carried on a desperate struggle in the Caucasus in support of the Provisional Government, demanding the dissolution of all the Soldiers' and Workmen's Councils by armed force and the immediate hanging of all Bolsheviks. By unascertainable methods he entered the Communist Party, and to-day he is still hanging men — but now anti-Bolsheviks!

III. HORRORS OF TIFLIS PRISON

Prince Mukhransky's Resolve — The Metekh — In the Hands of
Sadists — A Shunned Locality — "Shooting Nights" — A Biter Bit.

Among the thousands of persons imprisoned in the gaols of the
Trans-Caucasian Tcheka at the same time as myself were fifteen offi-
cers, among them General Tsulukudze, Prince Khimshieff, and Prince
Mukhransky, whose brother was married to the daughter of the Grand
Duke Constantine Constantinovitch. They were all charged with organ-
ising a mythical counter-revolutionary plot and being concerned in the
Georgian rebellion of 1923, and after prolonged, torturing examinations
were sentenced to be shot.

Prince Mukhransky resolved not to sell his life cheaply. He succeeded in getting hold of a large nail, found in the room. When, on
the night appointed for the execution, the door opened and a party of
Tchekists headed by Schulman, Commandant of the Trans-Caucasian
Tcheka, known as the "Death Commandant," entered to fetch away the
condemned officers, Mukhransky flung the nail as hard as he could into
Schulman's face, aiming at his eyes. The heavy nail broke the executioner's
nose. Schulman groaned with pain. At once an incredible noise arose. The
whole prison was awakened by cries and shots. The room was filled with
smoke. All the fifteen officers were killed on the spot by the escort. The
prisoners in other rooms were ordered to wash away the streams of blood.

The executioner Zlieff, plenipotentiary extraordinary in Ossetia of
the Gpu of the Mountain Republic, used to force the muzzle of a revolver
into the mouth of the prisoner he was examining and turn it about so
that it crushed the gums and knocked out teeth. My cell companion in
the prison of the "Gor-Gpu" was subjected to this torture. He was an old
Ossetian, who was accused of the following offence (to quote from the
indictment itself):

"The accused once walked past Tchelokaeff's[7] door."

* * * * * *

After a few weeks I was transferred to the chief prison in the Caucasus
— the Metekh[8] at Tiflis. As at the present day, the Metekh was used in 1923
as a place of detention for political prisoners only; ordinary criminals were

---

7   See Chapter I.
8   See Chapter I.

lodged in the Government prison. There were in the castle 2,600 "White Guards," including a large number of Georgian Mensheviks.

Inhuman reprisals were carried out methodically on these defenceless people — I saw many old men, women and children. Once a week — on Tuesdays — a special commission, consisting alternately of members of the Trans-Caucasian Tcheka and the Georgian Tcheka, sat in the commandant's office in the prison and drew up a list of victims, paying no more regard to the degree to which, in each case, proof of guilt existed than to the voice of humanity. The whole personnel of the castle, the "Zaktcheka" and the "Gruztcheka," was filled with sadists.

Every week, on Tuesday nights, from sixty to three hundred persons were shot in the prison. That night was veritable hell for the whole Metekh. We did not know who was marked down to be shot, so everyone expected to be shot. Nobody could get a wink of sleep till morning. The ceaseless bloodshed was a torture not only to the prisoners, but to people living in freedom outside. All the streets round the Metekh had long been uninhabited; the population of this quarter had abandoned their houses, unable any longer to listen to the shots of the executioners, the shrieks and groans of the victims.

The Tchekists in the Metekh were always drunk. They were regular butchers. Their resemblance to butchers was heightened by their habit of rolling up their sleeves to the elbow and walking through the corridors and cells, sometimes tumbling to the floor, drunk with wine and with human blood.

On "shooting nights" from five to ten men were taken from each room. The procedure of reading out the list of those doomed to die was drawn out by the Tchekists to an average minimum of a quarter of an hour in each room. There was a long pause before each name was read, during which the whole room shivered with terror. Even people with strong nerves could not withstand such torture. On Tuesday nights half the prisoners in the castle sobbed till morning came. Next day no one could eat a morsel of food; the prison dinner was left untouched. This happened every week. And prisoners from the Mountain Republic who came to the Solovky in 1925 told us that it was still happening then. Many people could not endure the prolonged nightmare and became insane. Many committed suicide, in every conceivable manner.

While I was in the castle a well-known Tiflis Tchekist, Zozulia, a Cossack from the Kuban, was placed among the prisoners to act as an agent provocateur. This executioner, in a comparatively short space of time, had shot over six hundred persons with his own hand — a fact which he did not deny. At last he was recognised and killed by the prisoners.

* * * * * *

I spent four months and a half in the Metekh, and prepared myself for death every Tuesday.

Then began an endless series of journeys and fresh prisons. From the Metekh I was transferred to the Government prison at Tiflis, thence to the "Timakhika" prison at Baku, where I spent a fortnight, then to the Tcheka prison at Petrovsk (three weeks), thence to Grozny, and from Grozny in "Stolypin trucks," specially constructed for prisoners, to Vladikavkaz. Everywhere was the same total suppression of human personality, the same torture by nocturnal interrogations, starvation and blows, the same lawless, indiscriminate shootings.

IV. BOUND FOR THE "SOLOVKY"

Finally "Amnestied!" — The "Shpana" — A Lucky Escape — Classification of Prisoners — Madame Kameneff's Protegees.

At last, on November 30th, 1923, i.e., seven months after I had been "amnestied" by the Batoum Tcheka, the examining judge of the Vladika-vkaz Tcheka finally "amnestied" me in the following terms:

"By order of the administrative exile commission of the People's Commissariat for Home Affairs, Citizen S. A. Malsagoff, having been found guilty of offences against the State of the nature contemplated by Clauses 64 and 66 of the Criminal Code of the R.S.F.S.R. — Clause 64, 'organisation of terrorist acts in co-operation with persons outside Russia,' and Clause 66, 'espionage for the benefit of the international bourgeoisie' — is exiled to the concentration camp in the Solovetsky Islands for a term of three years."

I and several others who had been "amnestied" were sent north by easy stages. The first halting-place was Rostoff. Here I first met face to face the so-called shpana — the ordinary criminals who play so singular a rôle in all the Russian prisons, camps and places of exile.

Robbers on a large and a small scale, burglars, murderers, horse-thieves, coiners, vagabonds — are flung in whole divisions from one prison to another, serve their term or escape by bribing their guards, but soon get into gaol again. Almost all are completely destitute of clothing, always starving, and covered with lice. The guards beat them over the head with their rifle butts, they murder one another with bricks wrenched out of the prison walls. Completely bestialised, wherever they go they gamble away their modest payok (food ration) and their last pair of trousers at cards. This loss they make good by robbing newly-arrived prisoners belonging to the political categories. The stolen things are sold through the overseers of the prisons and camps, and the money obtained for them is spent on drink.

On entering the room allotted to us in Rostoff prison, I was struck dumb with consternation; we were met by nearly a hundred shpana with deafening yells and menacing cries. In a corner sat five men of the educated classes, including a colonel on the General Staff; the shpana had stripped them naked in one night.

Luckily there were men among us who had been through every

imaginable experience. One of them drew a chalk line on the floor, dividing the room into two spheres of influence, political and criminal, and shouted to the shpana:

"If one of you crosses this line, I'll kill him!"

He was a man of gigantic stature; the shpana were intimidated. When night came, we posted sentries on the frontier of our sphere of influence. But for events taking this turn, the money and other things which our relations had managed to send us when on the way to Rostoff — by means of substantial bribes to the guards — would have been stolen from us.

From Rostoff we were sent to the Taganka in Moscow.

In the Taganka prison a noticeable degree of system prevails. There are separate rooms for "criminals" of different categories. In Moscow we made the acquaintance of the curious division of all "criminals" by the Soviet authorities not into two classes, "counter-revolutionaries" and "shpana," as in the Caucasus and Southern Russia, but into three.

The first group, called "K.R.", comprises persons suspected of acts or propaganda of a Monarchist or, in general, a bourgeois, anti-Socialist tendency. In this comprehensive group you may meet an ex-Minister and an ex-doorkeeper, a young non-commissioned officer and a general, a big manufacturer and an assistant in a small shop, an ex-princess and her cook. The Soviet authorities allot to the "K.R." group the whole clergy en masse, without distinction of Church, the whole of the educated and semi-educated classes, all merchants and all officers.

To the second group, the so-called "politicals and party men," belong prisoners from the remnants of the pre-Revolution Socialist parties — Social Revolutionaries, Social Democrats, Anarchists, etc. — which have not yet been merged with the Communists.

The third category comprises the criminals proper, the so-called shpana.

The Soviet authorities maintain this same distinction in the Solovky and all the other concentration camps and places of exile or settlement.

In the Taganka we were placed in a room packed full of clerics. There were the Vladika Peter (Sokoloff), the Archbishop of Saratoff, the monks of the Kazan monastery, etc. Almost all were accused of concealing church treasures at the time when the Bolsheviks were robbing the churches to satisfy the needs of the Komintern.[9] These bishops, priests and monks, like us, were sent to the Solovky.

In Petrograd, where we arrived at the beginning of January, 1924, a group of twenty men, so-called "Casino-ites," were placed in the same room as ourselves in the "second passing-through prison," occupied exclusively by prisoners going on to some other place.

Not long before a fashionable gambling hell in Moscow for highly-placed Communists, called the Casino, had been shut on the ground of too high play, drunken orgies, immorality and debauchery. The unofficial head of this honourable institution was Madame Kameneff, wife of the President of the Executive Committee of the Moscow Government.[10] The Moscow Gpu, when closing the Casino, did not dare to arrest the spouse of the Communist Governor-General of Moscow, but the whole staff of the gambling hell, headed by the croupier Petroff, was sent to the Solovky for three years.

These fellows were also our companions on our journey to Kem. Subsequently the "Casino-ites," at the instance of Madame Kameneff, were sent from the Solovky to a voluntary settlement in the Petchersk region. Before our flight from the concentration camp I heard that Petroff and Co. were back in Moscow.

Convoys of prisoners are now sent north from Petrograd once a week, on Thursdays. On one of these Thursdays — January 14th, 1924 — I and a large number of other "K.R.'s," "politicals and party men," and shpana, left for the Solovky in prisoners' trucks.

---

9   The Third, or Communist, International.

10   i.e. Province.

PART II THE SOLOVETSKY ISLANDS

I. THE FORERUNNERS OF THE "SOLOVKY"

Conditions in Earlier Camps — The "White House" — 100,000 Shot — Mass Drownings — A Commission of Inquiry — Survivors Removed to Solovetsky Islands.

Until late in 1922, Kholmogory[11] and Portaminsk performed the function now discharged by the Solovky. When I reached the Solovky at the beginning of 1924, I met a number of men, the survivors of the "K.R." prisoners in the concentration camps at these places. They had been transferred to the Solovky in August, 1922. I should like to state briefly what these men, who had remained alive by a miracle, told me.

The concentration camps at Kholmogory and Portaminsk were established by the Soviet Government at the end of 1919. The people sent to them from every part of Russia had to live in hastily-run-up hutments. These were never heated, even at the height of winter, when in these far northern latitudes the thermometer often falls to -50° or -60° Celsius (90 to 110 degrees of frost Fahrenheit).

The prisoners were given the following ration: one potato for breakfast, potato peelings cooked in hot water for dinner, and one potato for supper. Not a morsel of bread, not an ounce of sugar, not to speak of meat or butter. And these people, driven by the pangs of hunger to eat the bark of trees, unable to stand from exhaustion, were compelled by tortures and shootings to perform hard labour — digging up tree-stumps, working in the stone-quarries, floating timber.

They were absolutely forbidden to correspond with their families in any way or to receive from them parcels of clothes or food. All letters were destroyed, food and other things sent were consumed or used by the camp guards.

After the defeat of the armies of General Denikin and General Wrangel, at the end of 1919 and 1920 respectively, captured White officers and men and civilian inhabitants of the territories wrested from the White armies — men, women and children — were sent to Kholmogory, convoy after convoy. And after the suppression of the Kronstadt rebellion in April, <u>1921, all the sail</u>ors taken prisoner by the Bolsheviks, about 2,000 in

11   On the Dvina, 46 miles S.E. of Archangel.

number, were sent there. The remnants of Koltchak's army, various Siberian and Ukrainian chieftains, peasants from the Tamboff Government who had belonged to Antonoff's bands, tens of thousands of members of the intelligentsia of all nationalities and religions, Kuban and Don Cossacks, etc. — all flowed in a broad stream to Kholmogory and Portaminsk.

The higher administration of these camps was appointed by Moscow and carried out the instructions received thence. The middle and lower personnel consisted of imprisoned Tchekists, who had been transported for too open robbery, taking of bribes, drunkenness and other breaches of duty. These fellows, having no one else on whom to avenge their removal from their lucrative duties in the Extraordinary Commissions of Central Russia, treated the prisoners in the camps with indescribable cruelty.

The assistant commandant of the Kholmogory camp, a Pole named Kvitsinsky, was particularly ferocious. This sadist-executioner has on his conscience the horrors of the so-called "White House," in the neighbourhood of Kholmogory. The "White House" was an estate abandoned by its owners, containing a white-painted building. Here for two years (1920-22) shootings took place daily at the direction of Kvitsinsky. The terrible reputation of the "White House" was doubled by the fact that the bodies of those executed were not taken away. At the end of 1922 all the rooms of the "White House" were filled with corpses right up to the ceiling. Two thousand sailors from Kronstadt were shot there in three days. The smell of the decomposed bodies poisoned the air for miles round. The stench, which never abated by night or day, stifled the prisoners in the camps and even made them faint. Three-quarters of the inhabitants of the town of Kholmogory were finally unable to endure it any longer and abandoned their homes.

Without the slightest doubt the Soviet Government knew of the horrors perpetrated at Kholmogory and Portaminsk; it could not help knowing. But, having an interest in the pitiless extermination of their opponents, real and supposed, the leaders of the Communist Party confined themselves to washing their hands of the whole business.

Executions were carried out at other places besides the "White House." The Tchekists used to come into the prisoners' enclosure and, having marked down the destined victims, point to one or another of the prisoners with the words: "One — two — three. . . . One — two — three. . . . "One" meant that the prisoner was to be shot the same day, "two" that he was to be shot to-morrow, and "three" the day after to-morrow. This was usually done when a fresh large party had arrived, and room had to be made in the camp for the newcomers.

According to the evidence of eye-witnesses, about 100,000 persons in all were shot at Kholmogory and Portaminsk. There is nothing astonishing in this figure, terrible as it is. For three years on end these camps constituted the chief prison of all Soviet Russia. To them, in addition to the large convoys, were sent, from every place in European and Asiatic Russia, all those whom it was for any reason undesirable or inconvenient to kill on the spot — for example, all those who had been "amnestied" by local Soviet authorities.

The executioners of Kholmogory and Portaminsk used another method of destroying their prisoners: they drowned them. Of a whole series of cases known to me I will mention only those which follow.

In 1921 four thousand former officers and soldiers of Wrangel's army were ordered to embark on board a barge, and the vessel was sunk at the mouth of the Dvina. The men who were able to keep themselves on the surface by swimming were shot.

In 1922 several barges were loaded with prisoners. The Tchekists sank some of them in the Dvina in sight of everyone. The unfortunate passengers on board the other barges, among whom were many women, were landed on one of the small islands near Kholmogory and shot down with machine-guns from the barges. Mass murders were carried out on this island very frequently. Like the "White House," it was heaped with bodies.

Those who escaped being shot the Tchekists hounded to death by compelling them to do work beyond their strength. The prisoners in receipt of the above-mentioned ration, among them old men and women, worked all round the clock. It was counted a piece of luck to find a rotten potato in the fields; it was greedily eaten on the spot, raw.

When the Tchekists noticed that the inhabitants of the region — Lapps, Zyrians and Samoyedes — were throwing bread to the crowd of prisoners as they passed their huts, they began to take them to their work by another route, through thick forest and marshes.

If a newly arrived prisoner was decently dressed, they shot him at once, in order to get his clothes sooner.

Early in the summer of 1922 a Kronstadt sailor who, by chance, had remained alive escaped from the Kholmogory camp. He succeeded in making his way to Moscow, where he used his former connections to obtain an audience of the "Vtsik"[12] (All-Russian Central Executive Committee), and said to Kalinin:

"Do what you like with me, but turn your attention to the horrors in the northern camps!"

At this time 90 per cent, of the prisoners had already been done to death. Communist humanity had been sufficiently proved, and the Vtsik, exchanging anger for clemency, lent a gracious ear to the escaped sailor's prayer. At the end of July, 1922, a commission started from Moscow for Kholmogory to inspect the Kholmogory and Portaminsk camps. Its president was one Feldman.

Feldman himself could not conceal his horror at what he saw and heard at these places. He had the camp commandants shot, and sent their assistants and the rest of the personnel to Moscow, nominally to be tried. All the Tchekists, however, were pardoned and placed in positions of responsibility in Gpu offices in Southern Russia. Fully understanding that the "White House" and its scores of thousands of corpses were a burden on the conscience of Moscow, Feldman determined to wipe out the traces of all that had happened there. He therefore ordered the place to be burned down.

Feldman's commission had been empowered by the Vtsik to amnesty the prisoners in both camps. Only the ordinary criminals, the shpana, however, received their liberty. None of the "counter-revolutionaries" were amnestied.

In August, 1922, the remaining "K.R.'s" were sent under a reliable guard from Kholmogory and Portaminsk to the Solovetsky Islands, via Kem.

---

12   Vserossisky Tsentralnyi Ispolnitelnyi Komitet.

II. FROM MONASTERY TO PRISON CAMP

The Famous Solovetsky Monastery — Its Wealth and Economic Strength — The Bolshevist Invasion — Destruction and Pillage — Organisation of the Solovky — The Camps and their Rulers.

The "Solovetsky" concentration camp received its name from the Solovetsky Monastery, founded in 1429 by Saints Sabbatius and Hermann, while Saint Zosima built the first church in 1436. The island, seventeen miles long by eleven broad, on which the monastery stands, is one of a group known by the collective designation Solovetsky Islands; there are, besides the principal island, five other large ones — Ansersk, Great and Little Zajatsk, Great and Little Muksalm — and a number of small ones. They lie in the White Sea, at the entrance to the Gulf of Onega, and close to the western coast of the Archangel Government.

The Solovetsky Monastery, one of the most ancient and most held in honour of Russian monasteries, has long been noted for the peculiar asceticism of the life led by its inmates, the incalculable wealth of its churches and the large number of monks in the brotherhood, which is indicated by the fact that the number of boys sent by their relations to the monastery for a year reached in some years the figure of two thousand.

The monastery had, among other things, its own tannery, iron foundry, paper mill, match factory, saw mills, dozens of workshops of various kinds, a printing works (the workmen were all monks), a dock, a merchant fleet, and even a small navy for the defence of its shores. The monastery's infantry and artillery, consisting exclusively of monks, were also designed to serve this purpose.

The first years of the Revolution affected the organisation and economic strength of the monastery only to an insignificant degree, lying, as it did, to one side of the main road of Bolshevist pillage. Even at the time when the British were in these parts — it will be remembered that the Archangel and Murmansk areas were for a time occupied by a Russian anti-Soviet army, under General Miller, and British troops — the monastery still lived its old industrious life.

MAP OF NORTH-WESTERN RUSSIA, SHOWING THE
SOLOVETSKY ISLANDS.

The Soviet power destroyed this highly cultured advanced post of Russia in the Far North with characteristic violence and cruelty. In the autumn of 1922 all the wooden buildings of the monastery were burnt. The Bolsheviks began by murdering half the monks, including the Igumen of the monastery; the remainder they sent to forced labour in Central Russia. The treasures were plundered by the first Tchekists who entered the precincts. The decorations of the ikons were torn off, the ikons themselves blasphemously chopped up with hatchets for fuel. The bells were flung down from all the belfries and the fragments sent to Moscow to be melted down.

Besides a multitude of objects precious in a religious and material sense, the Soviet Huns destroyed treasures of immense historical value. The Tchekists pillaged the library of the monastery, which during the five centuries of its existence had been filled with unique works. They heated the stoves with rare books, old documents and chronicles of the greatest antiquity. Finally, the dishonest methods of the new management, combined with the criminal plundering and inexperience of the Soviet administration, ruined the factories and workshops belonging to the monastery.

The ancient building was reduced to a heap of ruins. The Tchekists put up a barbed wire fence round it. The half-destroyed Kremlin, or main enclosure of the monastery, became the headquarters of the "Slon."[13] All the branches of the Solovky are under the direction of the office in question, viz., the Solovky camp itself, the Kem camp (on Popoff Island), the camp on Kond Island, and the places of exile in the Petchersk and Zyriansk regions.

The Kem camp on Popoff Island (about a quarter of a mile from the shore and six miles from the town of Kem) is a base depot for the Solovky. In it are assembled, until navigation opens, thousands of new prisoners bound for the Solovky from all parts of Russia. The ordinary criminals who from time to time are amnestied are sent there from Solovetsky Island on their way south. Prisoners are continually being sent from the Kem camp to the monastery and from the monastery to Popoff Island for labour purposes — generally the latter, for most of the work is done on Popoff Island.

Before proceeding to a detailed account of the administration of the Solovky, I may mention that when I arrived in the domain of the Slon

13   Severnye Lageri Osobennavo Naznatchenia (Northern Camps for Special Purposes). Slon means "elephant" in Russian; the double entendre cannot, of course, be reproduced in English.

there were in the concentration camps over five thousand prisoners of the three categories defined in a previous chapter — "K.R.'s," "political and party men," and "shpana," or ordinary criminals.

In the monastery itself, the "K.R.'s" and criminals live in the cells and churches of the Kremlin which have escaped destruction, the "politicals and party men" in the hermits' caves which are scattered all over the island — three, six or eight miles from the Kremlin. On Popoff Island the prisoners are housed in hutments erected by the British — the "K.R.'s" and shpana together, the "politicals and party men" separately.

The supreme head of the administration of the Northern Camps for Special Purposes is a Moscow Tchekist, a member of the Vtsik, named Gleb Boky. (One of the Solovetsky steamers, by the way, has been re-named Gleb Boky in his honour.) He is a tall, thin man, apparently well educated. His bearing is generally gloomy, his eyes piercing; he always wears military uniform. He is the typical rigid Communist of superior education, with an element of cruelty in his disposition. He lives in Moscow, where he has some other employment in the Gpu, and only comes to the Solovky now and then.

His deputy, who lives permanently in the Kremlin of the monastery, is the real head of the Slon in practice; the fate of the prisoners in the Solovky is completely in his hands. His name is Nogteff. He is also a member of the Vtsik, and was formerly a sailor in the cruiser Aurora. He is semi-educated, drunken, and rather deaf, with a conspicuously cruel physiognomy. He is universally known in the camps by the nickname palatch (executioner). When he goes round the hutments and caves of the "political and party" prisoners, they shout in his face "Go away, executioner!" (I will explain later how it is that they are able to do this with impunity.)

Nogteff's right-hand man and deputy is an Estonian Communist named Eichmans. He suffers from "paradomania." Of smart military bearing himself, he demands the same of prisoners in a state of permanent starvation. They are compelled to salute him. Immediately on his arrival in the Solovky he began to teach the prisoners, with blows when required, how to reply to his "good morning" in a brisk, military tone, at the same time coming to attention.

When I arrived in the Solovky, and until March, 1924, the commandant of the "Kemperraspredpunkt"[14] was one Gladkoff, a Tchekist, born

14   This appalling portmanteau word, a fine flower of Soviet officia phraseology, signifies Kemsky peresylotchno-raspredelnitelnyi punkt (Kem

at Kaluga, in Central Russia, and formerly a workman. He was notable for his open peculation of Government money and his astounding patronage of the shpana. Almost illiterate, coarse, addicted to cards and drink, he was really in no way different from these common criminals. It was thus on what might be termed ideological grounds that Gladkoff established and strengthened the dictatorship of the shpana over the "K.R.'s" and politicals, and all the violence we endured at their hands.

---

distributing centre for prisoners passing through). These long-winded official designations, of no interest to the general reader, are given here for the benefit of students of Soviet Russian affairs.

III. A GALLERY OF TCHEKISTS

Convicted Tchekists as Prison Staff — The "Public Prosecutor" — A Foreign Visitor's Fate — Bela Kun's Right Hand Man — "Smolensky Sticks" — Moscow Prison Riot — The "Mother" of the Criminals — An Unpunished Peculator.

In March, 1924, a so-called "change of cabinet" took place. I will speak of this later, and continue my portraits of the ministers in the earlier combination.

Boky, Nogteff, Eichmans, Gladkoff — these were the men who had the power. They were sent to the Solovky from Moscow by Dshershinsky himself. The remainder of the personnel of the Solovetsky and Kem camps were Tchekist prisoners. There were several dozen of these at the monastery and on Popoff Island. When the corruption, fraud, violence or swinish drunkenness of Gpu officials cannot possibly be concealed from the public eye, they are brought to account for their offences without delay. Some are transferred to other places, some are sent for terms of from two to ten years to the Slon camps, where they are still employed in their "special branch."

I mention a few of the transported Tchekists who held, and still hold, important posts in the administration of the Solovetsky Islands.

Nogteff's assistant on the administrative side is one Vasko, a brutal villain. This individual is the "public prosecutor" of the Solovetsky Islands, and all the documents relating to the cases of the transported persons are in his hands. The importance of his function is due to the fact that, although all the "K.R.'s" and politicals are regarded as having been sentenced by the Gpu (always in their absence, without any kind of trial) and the term of their imprisonment is definitely fixed, in reality they are all in the position of persons whose cases are sub judice. At any moment new evidence can be discovered relating to their cases, with the result that their term of imprisonment may be extended, or they may be shot. Comrade Vasko's occupation is to search carefully for any fresh fact or allegation which may chain the prisoner to the Solovky more firmly and for a longer time; and in doing so he does not shrink from such methods as the employment of agents provocateurs, the blatant forgery of new "proofs," and so on.

The management of the technical side of the actual Solovetsky camp is in the hands of Roganoff, an engineer, sent to the Solovky for offences relating to the discharge of his functions. I do not know how he manages the affairs of the camp, but it is manifest to everyone that Mr. Roganoff, now that he has turned his coat, is in no way different from the real Tchekists, either in his behaviour towards the prisoners or in his self-indulgent manner of living. His technical assistants, both at the monastery and on Popoff Island, are engineers recruited from among the prisoners. They are people of no importance, almost as helpless against injustice and ill-treatment as all the rest of us.

The direction of the Northern Camps for Special Purposes is compelled, for reasons I will speak of later, to be self-supporting. It, therefore, concludes agreements of various kinds for the construction of roads and buildings with prisoner labour, wood-cutting, etc., with the Karelian Republic and with various economic organs of the central Government. It is also endeavouring to get the ruined factories and workshops on Solovetsky Island into working order again. Although all this, as will be shown later, results in nothing but confusion, the "Natchuslon"[15] has at his disposal something in the nature of a "juridical adviser in forced labour questions."

This, in practice, useless function is discharged Frenckell, a big Hungarian manufacturer. Frenckell came to Russia at the invitation of the Vneshtorg (Foreign Trade Office) to conclude a commercial treaty and take over certain Soviet enterprises on a lease by way of concessions. Instead of this he found himself sent to the Solovky for two years by order of the Gpu for "espionage for the benefit of the international bourgeoisie" (Clause 66 of the Criminal Code). Frenckell is sometimes ordered to Petrograd and Moscow on camp business of a commercial and juridical kind. The term of his punishment expires at the end of the present year (1925), but — by reason of the Gpu circular of August, 1924 — he will leave the Solovky not for Hungary, but for a further three years' stay, first in the Narym,[16] then in the Turukhansk[17] and finally in the Zyriansk region.

The lower administration of the Solovky consists of "starosty" (headmen), "commanders of labour regiments," and "commanders of labour companies."

Until recently the headman of the Solovetsky camp (who was also commander of a labour regiment) was a Tchekist named Michelson, a

15   Natchalnik Upravlenia Slona (Head of the Direction of the N.C.S.P.).
16   In Western Siberia, on the river Obi.
17   In North-western Siberia, near the mouth of the Yenisei.

lame misshapen creature of bestial ferocity. When the Soviet power was carrying out reprisals on the defeated Crimea, at the end of 1920 and the beginning of 1921, Michelson was the right hand of another wild beast, Bela Kun, the former dictator of the Hungarian Soviet Republic, whom he supported in his function of "President of the Triumvirate for the Conduct of the Red Terror in the Crimea." Michelson, like Bela Kun, became famous far beyond the frontiers of the Crimea for his executions of scores of thousands of Wrangel's officers and men and of the civil population. At last Dzerzhinsky himself, who could not possibly be suspected of humane motives, was obliged to put an end to the Crimean St. Bartholomew's Nights. Bela Kun was declared to be mentally abnormal and was recalled to Moscow (this was referred to in the Soviet papers), and Michelson was exiled to the Solovky. At the present date he is directing the activities of the Gpu in one of the "autonomous" Soviet republics.

Another personality worth noting is Marian Smolensky, a member of the Polish Communist Party, who when I arrived at the Solovky was commander of a labour company. In the middle of 1924 he was released from the Solovky and received a lucrative post in the Gpu. In the Soviet-Polish war of 1920 he was not taken prisoner, but went over to the Reds of his own accord. Proletarian "solidarity" was coupled in him with hatred of his fellow-creatures. He was a violent Polish Chauvinist, and hated the Russians so bitterly that he grew purple with rage at the very word "Russia." He was able to indulge his hatred with impunity at the expense of the prisoners, whom he beat without mercy. Smolensky's name has been perpetuated in the annals of the Solovky by the "Smolensky sticks" which he invented. These are thick curved cudgels, still used for flogging prisoners.

Another commander of a labour company, Grakholsky, must not be passed over in silence. He was shot at the Solovky in the autumn of 1924. Grakholsky declared that he had been an officer of the supply service under the Tsar, and gave the impression of being an intelligent man. He had only one eye. At the end of 1917, when the Bolsheviks seized power, he was appointed commandant of Oranienbaum, on the Gulf of Finland, and there he had his right eye knocked out, either by a bullet or by a rifle butt.

Grakholsky's chief claim to celebrity was the part he took in the famous rebellion in the Butyrka prison in Moscow in the winter of 1923. The prisoners, who had been kept in prison for years without any charge being brought against them, became desperate and started a rebellion under the direction of the politicals (Social Revolutionaries). One fine day all Moscow was awakened by wild yells. The prisoners, three thousand in number, disarmed the inner guard of the prison, smashed all the windows, and demanded that their cases should be dealt with immediately by Kalinin, the president of the Vtsik, and the dismissal of the public prosecutor of the Republic, the notorious Armenian, Katanian. They hung out of the windows and yelled till all Moscow heard them, chanting: "We — want — Ka-li-ni-i-i-n! Ka-li-ni-i-i-n! We don't want Ka-ta-nian!"

The whole city flocked to the prison. The streets leading to it were packed with people, many of them cheering. Neither persuasion nor threats could stop the demonstration. The yelling went on for nearly two hours. At last the Gpu used force. Two regiments of Gpu special troops ("tchon")[18] broke down the resistance offered and forced their way into the prison. The Gpu exacted a cruel punishment for the rebellion. Its organisers were shot in the prison yard the same day; all the other prisoners were beaten with ramrods. There was no heating at all in the prison for a fortnight, although it was freezing hard and all the windows were broken; the prisoners had their blankets taken away from them and were put on "starvation rations." Some of the men, who had howled louder than the others, were sent to the Solovky for five years. Grakholsky was one of these. Vasto, however, declared, six months later, that he had not only yelled loudly, but had also been one of the instigators of the demonstration; and he was accordingly shot.

Kvitsinsky, who was sent to Moscow for trial by Feldman after the Kholmogory inquiry, is already known to the reader. He was not punished in any way for his hideous crimes and is now in the Solovky, perpetuating the glorious traditions of the "White House" and continually wielding the "Smolensky sticks."

Until the "change of cabinet" in the spring of 1924 the commandant of the Kem camp was, as I have mentioned, Gladkoff, the patron of the common criminals. They found an even more potent defender of their interests in Gladkoff's wife, a simple peasant woman from Kaluga, who had her husband completely under her thumb. Her official title was "administratrix," but the whole camp called her "Mother," the name given her by the grateful shpana. And she was in truth a mother to the criminals. She allowed them to do no work, released them from the cells, and shielded them when they robbed and maltreated the other prisoners. It was absolutely useless to complain to Gladkoff that the criminals had robbed you of your last pair of trousers. The commandant of the "Kem distributing centre" invariably gave the same answer, plus a few unprintable terms of abuse:

---

18   Tchasti Osobennavo Naznatchenia (Units for Special Purposes).

"I don't care if they do rob you. My shpana have got nothing, and you're bourgeois."

Under the regime of Gladkoff and "Mother" the criminals exercised a dictatorship in the camps; in fact, to this day they are a privileged caste, the aristocracy of the Solovetsky Islands.

The assistant of the Kem commandant until the "change of cabinet" was Klimoff, a Tchekist prisoner. Before he entered the service of Dzerzhinsky's institution he had been commandant of the Kremlin in Moscow, and later of Trotsky's train. On being transferred to the Gpu he displayed such brilliant capacities for receiving bribes that he soon began to take the bread out of the mouth of the president of the provincial Gpu in which he was employed, and his chief got rid of him by sending him to the Solovky for ten years.

Men of talent come to the front everywhere. At the Solovky, Klimoff continued to occupy himself with his speciality, taking bribes. The Casinoites[19] brought large sums of money with them to the realms of the Slon and received a further supply every month from Madame Kameneff. They simply showered money on Klimoff, and in return were continually being let off work of some sort.

In 1924, instead of being brought to trial, Klimoff was transferred to the Solovetsky Monastery to take over the duties of director of the "Vokhra"[20] (internal security service). A man named Provotoroff came to Kem in his place, but soon left again to become commandant of Kond Island, close to Popoff Island.

The assistant of Gladkoff and "Mother" on the economic side was a Tchekist prisoner named Mamonoff, a young man of twenty-two or twenty-three. He had been sent to the Solovky for ten years for the virtuous actions which all Tchekists commit — taking bribes, drunkenness and maltreating arrested persons.

Despite his youth, Mamonoff was a man of experience. By flagrant thefts of State property — which he used to tell people about when he was drunk —, fraud and incompetence, he ruined the Kem camp economically and got the accounts into hopeless confusion. The Moscow Tchekist Kirilovsky, who replaced Gladkoff at the end of March, 1924, refused to take the camp over unless Mamonoff's proceedings were inquired into by a special commission. A commission of inquiry was, therefore,

19   See Part I, Chapter IV.
20   Otriad vnutrennei okhrany.

appointed by the central Government, and spent five months going through Mamonoff's books and accounts, day after day. An appalling picture of waste, theft and fraud was revealed. But Mamonoff received no punishment.

IV. POPOFF ISLAND CAMP

Cold, Damp and Darkness — The Camp: its Geography and Amenities — Recent Improvements — Light Work for a High Bribe.

Nature herself is against the exiles. The Northern Camps for Special Purposes lie in the farthest north. The climate is severe and damp. Summer lasts only two months, or two months and a half. It is very late before the snows melt and spring comes. There are frequent gales, snowstorms, biting northerly and north-easterly winds. For three-quarters of the year the Solovetsky Monastery is completely cut off from the outside world. The long, dark winter is most oppressive, especially as the lighting in the huts is so poor. The damp from the Solovetsky marshes has an injurious effect on the health of the prisoners, worn out by hard labour.

The Kremlin of the monastery, surrounded by a high stone wall, reminds one of a fortress. In it the "K.R.'s" and shpana live in what once were the monks' cells, which they themselves have to provide with board-beds and tables, and to heat, and in the churches. The latter were plundered not long ago, and many of them have broken windows. Besides the principal ones (the Preobrajensky, Troitsky-Zosimo-Sabbatievsky, and Uspensky cathedrals, and the churches of St. Nicholas, St. Philip, and the Annunciation of the Holy Virgin) there are some ten other churches and chapels and numerous separate hermits' dwellings, in which the "politicals and party men" live. The Tchekists occupy the house of the Archimandrite and the best cells.

Popoff Island is about three miles long and two miles broad. The strait, a quarter of a mile wide, between it and the mainland is very shallow, so that it has been found possible to build a bridge over it, on wooden piles, for the narrow-gauge railway which connects the island with the town of Kem — a local branch of the Petrozavodsk-Kem-Murmansk line. The distance from Popoff Island station to Kem station — which is two miles from the town — is about eight miles; there is a halt on the way, nearer Kem. A wooden track, made of duck-boards laid down across the marshes, leads from the concentration camp to the island station, and similar tracks connect the various buildings.

On the eastern shore of Popoff Island are two wharves, the northern and southern. Only the latter is in use. It is about forty miles from Popoff Island to Solovetsky Island — twelve miles from Popoff Island to Rymbaki, and twenty-eight more on to Solovetsky Island. Between Popoff Island and Rymbaki the sea does not freeze in winter, but between Rymbaki and

Solovetsky Island it does. There are a lighthouse and stores on Rymbaki.

The factory of the "Severoles" (Northern Timber Company) is close to the southern wharf. Prisoner labour is employed in it. The Red soldiers of the 95th Division occupy two large buildings near the camp, close to the wood store.

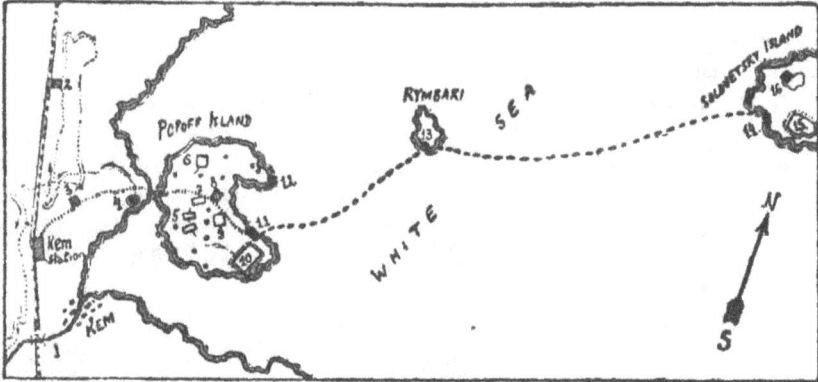

POPOFF ISLAND AND ITS SURROUNDINGS.

1. River Kem.
2. Railwayman's hut.
3. Railway halt.
4. Point from which our flight began—the dotted line shows our route during the first week.
5. Two buildings occupied by troops of the 95th Gpu Division.
6. Wireless station.
7. Wood store.
8. Popoff Island railway station.
9. Building of the *Severoles* (Northern Timber Company).
10. Concentration camp, surrounded by wire fence.
11. Southern wharf (in use).
12. Northern wharf (disused).
13. Lighthouse.
14. Wharf.
15. Solovetsky Monastery, surrounded by wire fence.
16. Sekirova hill, or Sekirka (place of punishment).

On the northern shore is the wireless station, in winter the sole means of communication with Solovetsky Island. The wireless station of the monastery is in the Kremlin. In clear weather the notorious Sekirova hill, on Solovetsky Island, can be plainly seen from the Popoff Island wharf.

The concentration camp is a rectangular enclosure some two hundred yards long and one hundred and fifty yards wide. It stands on a marsh at the south-eastern corner of the island, with heaps of stones scattered about it. The marsh promotes the spread of malaria, scurvy and lung complaints. The prisoners are fearfully tormented by the peculiarly poisonous mosquitoes of the Solovetsky Islands, which breed in swarms on the marsh and give one no peace either by day or by night.

The camp is surrounded by a high wire fence; along this, at intervals, stand huts for the sentries, each containing eight men. The Red soldiers in the guardroom outside the camp, generally thirty-eight in number, form a reserve force, to assist or replace the guards outside if needed. The Tchekists on duty are quartered in the commandant's office inside the camp.

All entrance to and exit from the camp is through the main gate, which is guarded by special sentries. The second gate (marked 11 on the plan) is kept permanently shut and is regarded as a reserve entrance.

Most of the huts in the camp were erected by the British troops which co-operated with the Russian Northern Army under General Miller. A few were constructed by prisoner labour under the Soviet regime. Until 1925 the camp possessed no latrine, hospital, electric power station, or workshops. There were no tracks, either of boards or of earth. Until quite lately the prisoners used to sink into the sticky slime of the marsh, and the huts were flooded with liquid mud.

The wooden tracks consist of boards and planks, supported by small piles sunk in the marsh. There are in all five of these roads or paths. The principal road runs from the main gate to the eastern side of the wire fence, and is called the Nevsky Prospekt. Others run from the reserve entrance to the Nevsky Prospekt, from the Nevsky Prospekt to the latrine, from the Nevsky Prospekt to hut No. 1 (marked 29 on the plan), where the politicals live, and from the last store hut to the hospital hut (marked 36 on the plan).

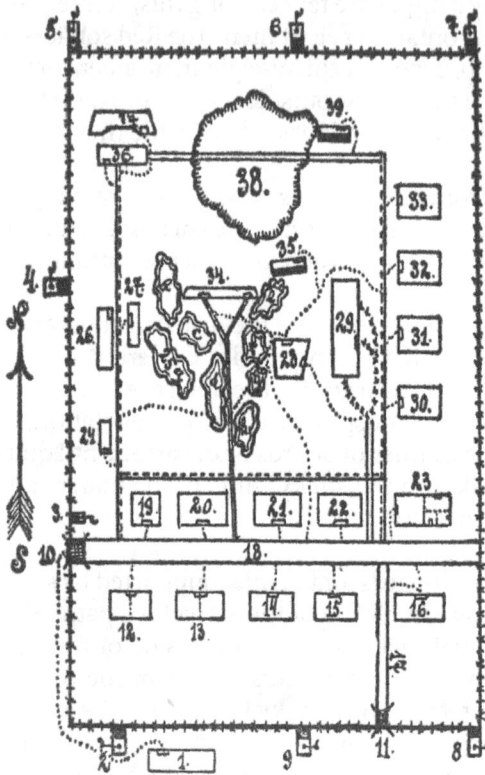

THE CAMP ON POPOFF ISLAND

1. Guard-room.
2-9. Huts for sentries (8 men in each) along wire fence.
10. Main gate.
11. Reserve gate.
12. Women's hut (in two compartments).
13. Camp clerks and Tchekists.
14. 2nd labour company.
15, 16. 1st labour company.*
20. Specialist labour company.*
21. 3rd labour company.*
22.   — *
17. Wooden track from reserve gate.
18. Nevsky Prospekt.
19. Commandant's office.
23. Prison, quartermaster on duty, etc.
24. Smithy.
25a, b, c, etc. Heaps of stones.
26. Workshops.
27. Electric power station.
28. Kitchen.
29. Politicals' hut.
30-33. Stores.
34. Latrine.
35. Refuse box.
36. Hospital.
37. Horses, carts, etc.
38. Ravine.
39. Hay store.

* " K.R.'s " and ordinary criminals.
Wooden tracks are indicated by double lines, earth tracks by single broken lines, and smaller paths by dotted lines.

Earth tracks run from the Nevsky Prospekt along the line of store huts (30 to 33 on the plan), from the Nevsky Prospekt past the kitchen, workshops, and electric power station to the hospital, and from the commandant's office past the huts where the shpana and "K.R.'s" are quartered. Besides these there are a few narrow, rough tracks through the marsh — from the politicals' hut to the kitchen, and elsewhere.

The commandant's office is in hut No. 2 (marked 19 on the plan). This hut is divided off into several compartments for the use of the various branches of camp government — administrative, economic, etc. The "specialist company," which is quartered in hut No. 4 (marked 20 on the plan), consists of tailors, bootmakers, joiners, and so on, who satisfy the requirements of the administration and the Red soldiers.

The electric power station is in charge of an engineer named Krassin. He was previously in the Customs service, but was dismissed for peculation and sent to the Solovky. The workshops are under an "adherent of Savinkoff," the kitchen is in charge of an ex-colonel named Rashevsky, and the stables of another "K.R." named Larin.

The business manager of the camp is one Pavloff (Nikolai Nikolae-vitch), a corrupt rascal. He takes bribes on the auction principle; he who offers most carries the day. I give one example. There is no water on Popoff Island; it has to be brought from Kem, and two carts with cisterns are kept for this purpose. As fetching water is easier work than digging up tree-stumps, there is great competition for this job. Pavloff asked openly who would give most for it. There were three prisoners who had managed to bring a good deal of money with them; they offered more than anyone else — 150 roubles between them — and they were still fetching water to the camp when I got away.

The higher camp authorities live in a small fishing settlement of about seventy cottages, a short distance outside the wire fence. The senior official on duty is quartered in the camp.

V. THE TYRANNY OF THE CRIMINALS

The "Distributing Hut" — Robbed the First Night — Criminals'
Unwritten Code — Punishment of a Traitor — The Professor's Parcel —
Successful Blackmail.

All newly arrived prisoners are sent first of all to the "distributing
hut" of the camp on Popoff Island.

Hardly have you set foot on the now accursed soil of the Solovky
before you feel the power of the shpana. When our party, consisting
of "counter-revolutionaries" from the Caucasus, bishops and monks, a
group of Casino-ites and many others, arrived at hut No. 6 (the "distributing hut"), we were met by armed Tchekists, themselves prisoners. They
wanted to know first of all whether there were any Gpu employees or
any criminal agents among us, for if so they might not go into the hut;
the ordinary criminals would kill them at once. Several men stood aside.

The rest of us entered hut No. 6. It was a huge wooden shed, filled
to overflowing with shpana. There were board-beds in two tiers, one
above the other. The beds and the floor under the lower tier were covered
with half-naked bodies. The stench was so awful that I nearly fell down.
Drunken yells and drunken weeping, the most disgusting abuse. There
was a feeble glow from a lamp in a corner.

I describe the "distributing hut" in some detail because all new arrivals have to go through this torturing stage of their captivity, and, further,
because nothing could be more characteristic of the whole conditions in
the Solovetsky camps.

Having been warned by our earlier experience at Rostoff, we lay down
on our things, putting them under our heads. But this precaution proved
to be inadequate. I was awakened during the night by a fearful noise. Star-
ing into the semi-darkness, I perceived with horror that all our things had
been stolen — our provisions plundered, our baskets, suitcases and boxes
broken open. Yells resounded from one corner, where one of the shpana
who had taken too much for himself was being sentenced to a beating
by an assize of his fellow-criminals. In another corner three criminals
were hitting one of their comrades over the head with pieces of wood;
he was dripping with blood, but still refused to give up the linen he held
tightly under his arm. On the upper tier of beds, close to the ceiling, the
national card game, tri listika, was already being played with our money.
At the door a knot of shpana were conducting trade negotiations with

the sentry, exchanging somebody's rug for spirits.

We "K.R.'s" decided next morning that it was useless to make a complaint. But one of the politicals in our party, a Social Revolutionary, indignantly told the commandant about the behaviour of the shpana who had left him with only one shirt in winter time. The commandant, for form's sake, appeared in the hut and called in timid tones:

"Give back the things! What disgraceful conduct!"

The criminals answered with a roar of laughter; but the next night they would have killed the "S.R." if we had not defended him.

Next morning an old inhabitant of the camp, Bishop Illarion Trotsky, the right-hand man of the late Patriarch Tikhon, was ordered to conduct our party to hut No. 9.

An unwritten internal discipline binds the ordinary criminals together. These starving, half-naked gallows-birds, dying by scores daily from scurvy and syphilis, never take a risk. The peculiar favour and protection which all the authorities of the Solovky, without exception, extend to the shpana is very simply explained.

The hostility which the ordinary criminal instinctively feels towards the "K.R.", the educated barin, is felt in an equal degree by every Tchekist in the Solovky, though he also sees in each "K.R." a counter-revolutionary, a Monarchist, a bourgeois. A further reason why complaints against the shpana are fruitless is that a large part of the Solovetsky administration are closely connected with the criminal classes, not only in their mentality, but in their pre-Revolution antecedents.

When I arrived at Popoff Island, there were about 1,400 shpana in the camp; the number of "K.R.'s" could have been divided into this total several times, and there were only seventy "politicals and party men." The last-named, for reasons which I will explain later, do no work at all, and "Mother" was continually letting the shpana off labour of all kinds, so that the whole immense burden of the work to be done was placed upon the shoulders of the "K.R.'s."

This is still the case, although in a lesser degree: the shpana do little work, the politicals none at all, and the "K.R.'s" bear the whole burden.

The criminals' curious code of ethics combines all the shpana of the Solovetsky Islands into one indivisible unit. This code of ethics is ruthlessly applied. If the criminals discover that there is a sutchenyi among their number — this word means in their language a turncoat, a traitor, who is betraying their secrets to the authorities — he is immediately put to death in the most cruel manner. Nowhere is the principle "one for all and all for one" put into application in so high a degree as among the common criminals of the Solovky.

In the middle of 1924 a gang of footpads, who had for a long time evaded all attempts to capture them, were arrested in Moscow. Their leader was a bandit named Moiseiko; his fellow-robbers nicknamed him Petlura, for which reason the members of the band were called "Petlurists." These footpads had on their conscience, besides a number of armed robberies, many "wet affairs" (a "wet affair" means a murder in the thieves' language). One of the most active of the Petlurists, known as Avrontchik, turned sutchenyi, betrayed the gang and brought about its arrest.

The gang consisted of thirty-eight persons, both men and women. Thirty of them were "sent to the left" (thieves' jargon for "shot") in the Butyrka prison in Moscow. Eight men, among them Avrontchik, and four women (the wives of men who had been shot) were despatched to the Solovky. When the "traitor" arrived at the "distributing hut," the surviving Petlurists burst in and almost beat him to death. The male Petlurists were arrested and Avrontchik taken to hospital. But he was not safe even in hospital; the four women of the band entered the hospital hut and killed Avrontchik, smashing in his skull.

The affair was referred to Moscow. The Gpu replied briefly: "shoot." In November, 1924, the remaining Petlurists, men and women, fell to Tchekist bullets, confirming by their death the principles of the shpana.

If the shpana do not shrink from murdering persons objectionable to them, much less does the robbing of all and sundry seem to them a thing to be boggled at. Further, they are compelled to rob by continual hunger, cold — in the Solovky one quite often sees shpana prisoners absolutely naked — and their passion for cards and drink.

Their robberies, the victims of which are invariably "K.R.'s," are planned with quite professional ingenuity. As I have said, on our arrival at Popoff Island we were moved from hut No. 6 to hut No. 9. This hut is divided into four compartments by wooden partitions. In the first compartment lived the headman of the camp, in the second the Casino-ites, the third was the camp prison, and in the fourth were we "K.R.'s," having a common wall with the prison.

Several times the shpana played the following trick on us. They committed some offence more serious than usual, and so, intentionally, got into the prison; then they bored a hole in the wooden wall which separated the prison from our quarters, quite close to the floor, and at night, creeping noiselessly under the beds, stole our things, food and money. If anyone tried to recover the things, they beat him to death.

The shpana always shared their plunder with the prison guards and the headman, so that nobody paid any attention to our complaints, and once the headman declared that we ourselves had robbed each other.

Sometimes the robberies were followed by impudent blackmail, also with the close connivance of the personnel. For example, among the prisoners in our hut was Professor Krivatch-Niemanetz, a very old man, over seventy. He was a Czech by nationality and had been employed in the Commissariat for Foreign Affairs as a translator. He was sent to the Solovky (for ten years) by virtue of that clause of the Criminal Code under which foreigners are always sent there — Clause 66, "espionage for the benefit of the international bourgeoisie." Of course he was absolutely innocent. Krivatch-Niemanetz was very popular in the camp and profoundly respected, mainly because he could speak nearly all the languages in the world fluently, including Chinese, Japanese and Turkish, not to mention all the European languages.

The Professor had received a parcel of things from the "Political Red Cross," which was presided over by Madame Peshkova, the wife of Maxim Gorky, and extended its help only to "politicals and party men." It evidently regarded "K.R.'s" as simply bandits, delivered as such to the caprice of Fate, the Solovetsky administration and the shpana.

He was as delighted with the parcel as a child, but alas! not for long. The shpana had got into the prison again; once more they broke through the wall and stole our things, including Krivatch-Niemanetz's parcel. In the morning the criminals had recourse to blackmail, a method of theirs by this time familiar to us all; they sent to the Professor — by a Tchekist — a letter in which they offered to give him back his things for 6 tchervontsy (about £6). The Czech, freezing in the draughty hut, accepted the offer as genuine despite our warnings, and sent the shpana — through the same Tchekist — all the money he had, leaving himself literally without a kopek. As we expected, he never got either his things or his money back!

Some time after this a number of the shpana left the Solovky, among them the men who had robbed the Professor. On their way south they sent him a letter in which they promised "never to forget the dear Professor to their last day."

The criminals regard stripping the "K.R.'s" almost as a point of honour, but stripping their own comrades, their fellow-criminals, as a crime to be severely punished. There is a special hut on Popoff Island in which all the parcels for the "K.R.'s" and politicals on Solovetsky Island received during the autumn and winter are kept until navigation opens and it is possible to communicate with the monastery; when spring comes they are sent to the monastery by a special steamer. Several times members of the shpana broke into this hut, enjoyed the fruits of their pillage with impunity and received the full approval of their fellows. But once, when a party plundered the hut at a time when some parcels for ordinary criminals were there, they were cruelly man-handled by their comrades and two of them actually killed.

VI. "COUNTER-REVOLUTIONARIES"

Hardest Labour Done by "K.R.'s" — Counter-revolutionary: a Comprehensive Term — A Variegated Multitude — Special Persecution of the Clergy — Prominent Clerical Prisoners.

On Solovetsky Island the "politicals and party men" live in separate cells — hermits' caves — and on Popoff Island in a special hut. Both at the monastery and in the Kem camp the "K.R.'s" live in company with the ordinary criminals. The cells of the monastery and the huts of the camps are filled to overflowing with a carefully mixed crowd of "counter-revolutionaries" and shpana.

The "K.R.'s" not only do all the hardest labour, and have to keep their own quarters clean, but are obliged to cleanse the criminals' bedsteads of dirt, remains of food, spittle and lice. Whenever a new party of "K.R.'s" arrive, they are compelled to clean out the huts, which the shpana have made so filthy that the task makes many of the "K.R.'s" sick. In 1924, it took 1,500 "K.R.'s" two whole months to clean out the camp on Popoff Island. It is sufficient to say that the criminals very often fulfil the requirements of Nature on the spot, i.e., in the huts.

The shpana, of course, are not in the least grateful for having all this done for them. On the contrary, this work of the "K.R.'s", so utterly degrading to human self-respect, is accepted by the criminals as a matter of course, and only exposes those who do it to fresh outrage from the shpana, supported by the camp personnel.

For example, when we had cleansed the hut indicated by the authorities of all the filth that was in it, the grateful shpana sent us an ultimatum, with a detailed schedule of the quantities of bread, sugar, tobacco, tea, etc., which were to be handed over immediately to the criminal who brought the ultimatum. If we failed to comply with the ultimatum, we were told, we should be first beaten and then plundered in more thorough fashion.

We had to hand over the things demanded. Ultimatums of this kind are very fashionable among the shpana; the "K.R.'s" are snowed under with them, both at the monastery and in the Kem camp.

It is very hard to give an exact account or analysis of the prisoners labelled "K.R.'s." Their number is considerable — there are nearly three thousand on Solovetsky Island — and they are composed of such variegated elements that a general definition of a "K.R." is very hard to arrive at.

A division of them into groups, even an approximate one, will enlighten the reader in a general sense as to who the "K.R.'s" are, and why they are in the Solovky, but it is bound to be incomplete; there are in the camps many "K.R.'s" whom one does not know where to place.

There are in the Northern Camps for Special Purposes many representatives of the so-called liberal professions — engineers, barristers, literary men, artists, teachers, doctors. There are many teachers from the primary and secondary schools and from the universities, both men and women; the latter are in a majority. There are a considerable number of non-party peasants and workmen, artisans and small employees. The Cossacks of the Don, the Kuban and Siberia, and the peoples of the Caucasus, are strongly represented. Of the non-Russians who are Soviet subjects the most numerous are Estonians, Poles, Karelians (some of those who returned from Finland on the strength of an "amnesty")[21] and Jews. The last-named are sent to the Solovky, in most cases with their families, either for adhering to Zionism, or for "economic counter-revolution," or for so-called "armed banditism" — by which the Gpu understands anything it pleases, from membership (even in the past) of a Monarchist party to the manufacture of counterfeit notes.

There are many foreigners in the Solovky; I will allude to them in greater detail later.

The largest categories of all consist of officers of the old and the new armies, business men, pre-Revolution and of the "Nepman"[22] order, important representatives of the old regime, the bureaucracy and the aristocracy, and also the clergy.

At the present time there are some three hundred bishops, priests and monks in the Solovky; to this number should be added several hundred laymen who were sent to the Solovky along with them, generally under Clause 72 of the Criminal Code — "ecclesiastical counter-revolution, resistance to the confiscation of church valuables, propaganda, the education of children in a religious sense," and so on. The clergy at the Solovky, though more oppressed and humiliated by the camp authorities than any other category of prisoners, are remarkable for the submissiveness and stoicism with which they endure their moral and physical sufferings.

---

21   They had taken refuge in Finland after the suppression by the Bolsheviks of the rebellion in Eastern Karelia at the beginning of 1922.
22   The term "Nepman" was applied to business men who grew rich under the "N.E.P." (New Economic Policy), introduced by the Soviet Government in 1922.

Being accustomed to hard bodily labour from childhood, the clergy are rightly considered to be the best workers in the camps, and from this point of view are almost valued by the administration, though it exploits them infamously. Priests are sent to do all the most exhausting tasks. For example, whole sections of the narrow-gauge railway were laid entirely by clerics.

All kinds of religious services, of course, are forbidden. One of the priests in the camp on Popoff Island, a feeble old man, died. He begged the commandant with tears in his eyes to allow the Vladika Illarion to administer the Holy Sacrament to him. The commandant refused in abusive terms.

Every day in the year is counted as a working day, and at Easter and Christmas the authorities endeavour to give the clergy the most degrading work possible — for example, cleaning out the latrines.

Among the most prominent clerics confined in the Northern Camps for Special Purposes are the following:

The Vladika Illarion (Trotsky), head of the diocese of Moscow and the right-hand man of the late Patriarch Tikhon. Neither when at liberty nor in prison has the Metropolitan Illarion ever entered into conflict with the Soviet power; but he has always been a vehement champion of pure Orthodoxy as a counterpoise to the "living Church," which is liberally subsidised by the Gpu. For the defence of his faith, and for his intimate connection with the Patriarch Tikhon, the bishop was sent to Archangel for three years and served his term of punishment under the most horrifying conditions. He returned to Moscow and again vigorously opposed the "living Church," took a skilful part in religious discussions, mercilessly shattered the Communistic babble of his opponent Lunatcharsky,[23] and was transported once more — this time to the Solovky.

The Vladika Masuil (Lemeshevsky) directed the affairs of the diocese of Petrograd after the shooting of the Metropolitan Venianin. Sentenced to transportation under Clause 72 of the Criminal Code — "ecclesiastical counter-revolution" — by which the Bolsheviks understand, inter alia, the defence of Orthodoxy against the destructive attacks of the "living Church," the bishop arrived at the Solovky in September, 1924. Six other bishops and monks and twelve laymen were sent there at the same time and for the same cause.

Bishop Seraphim (Kolpinsky), Bishop Peter (Sokoloff), Acting Bishop

23   People's Commissary for Education in the Soviet Government.

of Saratoff, and Bishop Pitirim (Kryloff), the Igumen of the Kazan Monastery, as well as about fifteen members of the black and white clergy from that monastery, were all sent to the Solovky under this same Clause 72. Hundreds of other bishops, priests and monks were transported, not only because the religion they professed was "opium for the people,"[24] but because they would not approve the plundering of the churches for purposes which had nothing to do with the relief of the famine victims, and which they denounced to the public as the work of the supporters of the "living Church," bought by the Government.

---

24   Lenin's phrase.

VII. THE TCHEKA'S VICTIMS: SOME STRANGE CASES

A Wife and her Husband — Annual "Amnesty" Swindle — Boris Savinkoff's Terrible End — Famine Relief a Crime — Dzerzhinsky in a New Light — An Indefatigable Vermin-hunter — Aged Hostages Tortured.

The grounds for which people have been transported to the Solovky are so various, and very often so completely baseless, that one cannot help supposing them to be pure inventions of the Tchekist "jurisprudence."

For example, among the prisoners there is the aged Countess Frederiks. During the war, as a Red Cross nurse, the old lady performed admirable service in tending wounded officers and men. And now, in the camp, she receives no parcels from the Red Cross, gives what help she can to the sick, and lives in a state of permanent semi-starvation, ceaselessly subjected to jeers and insults. She was transported for no other reason than that she had the misfortune to be the sister of Count Frederiks, who was Minister of the Imperial Court under the murdered Tsar, and was well-known as an intimate counsellor of Nicholas II. And while she was sent to the Solovky, the Count himself, a very old man of nearly a hundred, was until lately living in freedom in Petrograd; only quite recently was he given permission to leave for Finland.

In one of the cells on Solovetsky Island (the so-called Women's Building) the wife of a prominent minister of the old regime is perishing of under-nourishment and unaccustomed hard bodily labour. The official note of the decision in her case ran: "Transported to the Solovky for five years, as being the wife of a minister of Bloody Nicholas!" The minister himself fills a conspicuous post at Moscow under the Soviet Government!

A locksmith named Timoshenko was sent from Voronesh to the Solovky for two years. He was a simple workman and had had nothing whatever to do with politics. He continually endeavoured to obtain from Vasko an answer to his question — for what offence he had been sent to a concentration camp. Not till 1925, when his term of two years expired, was he accused of belonging to the "Savinkoff counter-revolutionary organisation" and sent to cool his heels for three years more in the Narym region.

At the same time other "Savinkoffists" were sent to the Solovky from Novokhopersk, a district town in the Government of Voronesh. They were: Vrashnikoff, former agent of Count Vorontsoff-Dashkoff's property in the Caucasus; Savinoff, a technician; Krivjakin, the business manager of a Soviet institution, and others. To these were added an engineer named Novitsky, from the Government of Poltava, and a crowd of peasants from the Government of Voronesh. Many of the peasants, when told at the Solovky that they were charged with complicity in "Savinkoff's conspiracy," asked doubtfully:

"Savinkoff?[25] Who's he? A general?"

When I was in the Solovky, one Epstein arrived there; he had been sentenced to three years. When he asked why he had been transported, he received from the examining judge the answer:

"Because you're a business man!"

Exactly the same answer was received by another criminal, a Jew tailor named Gurieff, who kept a ready-made clothes shop. (He is now in charge of the tailors' workshop in the Kem camp.)

Not long ago two Poles, named Minitch and Vintovsky, fled to Russia from Poland. The frontier authorities gave a ceremonial reception to the men, who had "escaped from cruel imprisonment by the Polish Pans," but the Moscow Gpu sent them to the Solovky for three years. The two Poles are now cursing the day when they decided to cross the frontier of the "freest Government in the world!"

Every year there arrive at Kem some two thousand "K.R.'s," who are sent on to Solovetsky Island when navigation is possible. The arrivals are especially numerous during the months which immediately precede November 7th (October 25th, old style), the date of the Bolshevist Revolution of 1917.

Every year at this time the Vtsik — thus controverting "the malignant lies of the international bourgeoisie and the shameless émigrés" about the cruelty of the Soviet power — publishes a wide amnesty to "all enemies of the ruling proletariat." The presidents of the provincial and district branches of the Gpu, by way of carrying out the directions of the humane Vtsik, shoot half their prisoners a few days before the amnesty and send the rest to the concentration camps, to which the terms of the amnesty decree state that it is not extended.

Thus, in reality, nobody is amnestied on November 7th. The Vtsik is satisfied, the Gpu is satisfied too; "the lies of the shameless bourgeoisie" have been exposed.

25   Boris Savinkoff, the well-known Social Revolutionary leader, see p. 109.

I could fill several pages with the names of people who have been "amnestied" in this manner. I will quote, as an example, a case in which not only the individual who was stupid enough to believe in the good faith of the Tchekists, but his relations too, were "amnestied." At the end of 1923 a soldier of Denikin's army, a peasant from the Government of Poltava, returned to Russia on the strength of the amnesty proclaimed by the Soviet Government in November of that year. He was given a Soviet passport on the frontier, and on arriving at his home went to the provincial Gpu, was registered, was sent away again and spent several days with his family.

Result — at the beginning of 1924 the soldier was sent to the Narym region of Siberia for three years, while his father and father's sister were despatched by the Gpu to the Solovky for concealing a counter-revolutionary (Clause 68 of the Criminal Code)! At the time of my escape these peasants, the victims of this singular "amnesty," were still in the Solovky, waiting to be sent on to the Zyriansk region.

"Amnestied" émigrés are continually being sent to the Solovky. Just before my escape a large party of émigrés arrived, nine-tenths of them private soldiers; there were a few officers, among them a cavalry subaltern named Menuel and Saprunenko, who had been aide-de-camp to the Ukrainian hetman Skoropadsky.

The Soviet power extends a real amnesty only to people, whether émigrés or living in Soviet Russia, whose names can be used later as a decoy. Such gentlemen, for example, as ex-General Slastschoff and similar renegades can live in freedom and even occupy responsible posts so long as this suits the book of the Gpu, so long as the Gpu reckons that it can make use of the name of one of these "signal-changers"[26] to prove "the good faith of the Soviet power, which amnesties all repentant émigrés." But as soon as the renegade in question has "done his job," he can go away, or, to be more correct, he is sent away, to exile or to the next world. It is sufficient to recall the fate of the well-known Social Revolutionary Savinkoff, who was "amnestied" by the Bolsheviks — after which the Tchekists flung him from a fifth-floor window of his prison.

Ordinary émigrés who return are immediately sent to the Solovky or the Narym region — that is to say, if the "supreme measure of punishment" (shooting) has not already been applied to them. The latter fate,

26 Smienoviekhovtsy, "signal-changers" — a name popularly given to people, formerly of anti-Soviet opinions, who have changed their political course and become reconciled to the Bolshevist Government.

as a rule, awaits officers.

The Soviet Government, returning evil for good, sends to the concentration camps people who have "besmirched themselves" by working with organisations of which the unhappy Russian people will always retain a grateful memory. Among the prisoners at the Solovky is a dentist named Malivanoff, a Moscow Jew. Malivanoff gave active help to the A.R.A. (the American relief organisation for the benefit of the famine victims), with the result that he was sent to the Solovky for five years. As the Criminal Code of the U.S.S.R. does not at present provide any punishment for giving relief to famine victims, the clause relating to "economic espionage" was applied to Malivanoff! A number of other Russians who worked with the A.R.A. and famine relief organisations from other countries were sent by the grateful Gpu to Siberia, to the Narym and Petchersk regions.

Karpoff, well known as the stage manager of the Alexandrinsk Theatre in Petrograd, and subsequently of the Great and Little Theatres in Moscow, was sent to the Solovky in company with other artists — Jurovsky, Georges, etc. — on the charge of "counter-revolution." During my stay there he was sent on to another place of exile.

If the Tchekists want to transport somebody, but cannot find a handle for doing so, Clauses 68 ("concealing a counter-revolutionary") and 72 ("ecclesiastical counter-revolution") serve their purpose most conveniently.

One of the most peculiar cases is that of a man named Witte, from Petrograd, who was transported because he bore "a counter-revolutionary name!"

There are Communist engineers — e.g., one Osipoff, who was famous throughout the camp for the incredible quantity of lice on his body — naval officers who had been "seksoty,"[27] jewellers, hair-dressers, landowners, followers of Makhno (the Ukrainian guerilla leader), "economic bandits," commanders of the Gpu troops, watchmakers — in short, prisoners of every conceivable profession, position, rank and designation.

The case of the brothers Myshelovin, watchmakers, was a curious one. They were both accused of forging and uttering notes, although the evidence given before the examining judge and the results of a domiciliary visit showed that while one of the two brothers had actually uttered counterfeit notes, the other was completely innocent. And what was the decision of the Gpu? It sent the guilty brother to the Solovky for three

27   Sekretnye sotrudniki; secret collaborators (with the Gpu).

years — and the innocent one for ten years!! The motives of Tchekist "courts" in pronouncing such sentences as this must always be a mystery to us all.

A very interesting figure was the technical engineer Krasilnikoff (Nicholas Dimitrievitch). He had been sent to the Solovky for "ecclesiastical counter-revolution," but in reality he had had no connection with anything of the kind. Before the Revolution he had been well known in Petrograd as an able and vehement opponent of Socialism of all shades. When the Bolsheviks came into power, Volodarsky sent for him several times and tried to persuade him to stop preaching counter-revolution. But the truculent engineer, taking advantage of his immense authority among the workers, continued to make speeches and publish his pamphlets. He soon migrated to Moscow and there continued his activities, the tendency of which was, as in pre-Revolution days, to discredit Socialism of all kinds.

Dzerzhinsky himself was interested in Krasilnikoff and sent for him. The engineer appeared at the Gpu headquarters, and there, in the study of the President of the Extraordinary Commission, Dzerzhinsky and Krasilnikoff disputed for hours on end about Socialism and its Utopian aims. It must have been almost the only time in his life that Dzerzhinsky permitted freedom of speech — and that in the very offices of the Gpu! Krasilnikoff — a brilliant speaker — endeavoured to persuade the head Tchekist to abandon all hope of being able to make a reality of such nonsense as Socialism. Dzerzhinsky would not agree, but put forward arguments on the other side.

The night wore on. Dzerzhinsky offered the engineer a camp bed in his study, and in the morning ordered that he should be given coffee and allowed to go. Soon after, however, he was arrested by subordinate Tchekists and sent to the Solovky.

In the camp, Krasilnikoff was literally eaten up by lice. I myself, having passed through dozens of prisons on my way north, possessed the experience of a lifetime in the matter of vermin; but never and nowhere have I seen such multitudes of lice as on the engineer. Every morning and every evening he used to kill vermin in incredible quantities, remarking every time he caught one:

"Aha, got him — that's another!"

The Solovky swallow up old and young alike. In February, 1925, fifty students and schoolboys from Theodosia, Sevastopol, Simferopol and Yalta, in the Crimea, arrived at Popoff Island. They had all got three years for organising a "counter-revolutionary conspiracy in complicity with the foreign bourgeoisie." The latter was alleged to be directing the conspiracy from Constantinople, but the whole thing was quite unproved. Besides adult students, the party included some twenty pupils of the middle and upper classes in the secondary schools, quite boys still.

Not long before I came to the Solovky, the Gpu of the Trans-Caucasian Soviet Republic had sent thither forty Tchetchentsy,[28] very old men. One of them looked out of the window of a hut, which is forbidden by some Tchekists, on which the whole party were sent to the Sekirova hill — notorious at the Solovky as the place of torture —, put into "stone sacks" (an operation described in a later chapter) and flogged with "Smolensky sticks" till they fainted. One of these aged men was 110 years old.

These old Tchetchentsy had been transported as hostages for their sons, grandsons and great-grandsons who had joined guerilla bands and were waging a ceaseless war with the Bolsheviks — a war which is still going on. They themselves had not committed any kind of offence.

The practice of taking hostages, and of carrying out violent reprisals on the relations and even the acquaintances of rebels and émigrés, has been developed by the Soviet power into an elaborate system of terror, which shrinks from nothing that may help it to attain the object in view — the submission of the entire Russian people to the will of the leaders of the Communist Party.

---

28   A Caucasian nationality.

VIII. "POLITICALS": A FAVOURED CLASS

Modern Cave Dwellers — Why They are Better Treated — Cultural Privileges — Socialists' Courage and Discipline — Hunger Strikes — Common Criminals "Unloaded" — A Remarkable Soviet Pamphlet.

The "politicals and party men" on Solovetsky Island at the present time number about five hundred, including a hundred and fifty women and several dozen children. Children are placed on the same footing as adult prisoners as regards rights and obligations, and so receive rations. On Popoff Island there are now sixty male politicals and twenty women. Most of them are members of the Social Revolutionary, Social Democratic, "Bund" and Anarchist parties, and intermediary shades, transported to the Solovky for active opposition to the Soviet power in the years 1917-19 and passive criticism of its actions in the years that followed.

Solovetsky Island is roughly forty miles in circumference and is rich in caves, inhabited in bygone days by religious monks, hermits and holy men vowed to silence. These caves, cut in the rock, recall mediæval country houses. They are scattered about the island, the distance from the monastery varying from three to six or even ten miles. Here the politicals are settled in parties, twenty or thirty persons in each cave.

In the Kem camp they live in a special hut, No. 11 (marked 29 on the plan), which is divided into two rooms, one for the men and one for the women and children. The hut is surrounded by a wire fence and is guarded by special sentries.

On Solovetsky Island the "politicals and party men" can walk about the island and visit each other quite freely, without guards. On Popoff Island they are taken out for exercise with a sentry, not accompanied by "K.R.'s" or ordinary criminals.

Standing much closer, in their ideology, to the Bolsheviks (if the Bolsheviks can be said to have any ideology) than the "K.R.'s" do, the politicals naturally receive a certain consideration from the Soviet authorities and have some attention paid to their needs and demands. In this respect the Soviet power is influenced partly by the right wing of the Communist Party and to a considerable extent by the Socialists of Western Europe, to whose utterances the Communists, despite their assertions to the contrary, listen attentively. The result is that while it sends "politicals and party men" to places of exile, it keeps them there under conditions which are paradise compared to the quite insupportable existence of the "K.R.'s" in the Solovky and in the other concentration camps.

It was not till after the "change of cabinet" in the spring of 1924 that the "K.R.'s" were permitted to correspond with their relations — the letters being carefully read by the Tchekists — and to receive parcels from them. The politicals have always enjoyed these rights.

If a "K.R." has no relations, or his relations are not in a position to send him money, food and other necessaries, he is doomed to death from starvation, for the camp ration, issued for ten days in advance, is sufficient for two days only. In this connection, it should not be forgotten that the Gpu, when it sends a "K.R." to a place of exile, generally confiscates all the property belonging to him and his family. The politicals receive everything they need in abundance, not only from their relations, but also from (1) the "Political Red Cross" presided over by Madame Peshkova,[29] (2) from foreign Socialist organisations, which send help on a most generous scale, and (3) from the "committee for the assistance of Russian prisoners and exiles." It must be emphatically stated that the "K.R.'s" did not once receive any help from this body.

The politicals have their own library, which is continually supplemented with new Russian and foreign books. They are allowed to subscribe to Soviet newspapers and foreign journals of a non-political character. They are allowed to form societies for cultural purposes. The leaders of the politicals read papers on various questions and organise debates, both in the caves and in hut No. 11. The politicals are allowed to occupy themselves with sport. The administration listens attentively to any complaints they may make.

The "K.R.'s" have no advantages of the kind. The camp reading-room is at their disposal, but as the shpana periodically turn it into a latrine, no "K.R." ever puts his nose inside it. Two publications are received in the camps, the newspaper Bednota (Poverty) and the periodical Bezbozhnik (The Godless One), but even this literature the "K.R.'s" do not get hold of until two or three months after its arrival, for it is read first by the Kem administration, then by the Solovetsky administration, and then by the Red soldiers. Of course, the "K.R.'s" are not allowed to carry on any work of a cultural, let alone a political nature, and in any case they would have no time, ceaselessly occupied as they are with work beyond their strength. How the administration treats complaints from "K.R.'s" the reader knows already. Finally, the politicals, according to established tradition, do no work at all, which is at the same time an immense privilege and an atrocious injustice. All the work, both "outside" (outside the

29   Maxim Gorky's wife, see p. 92.

camps) and "inside" (inside the camps), falls on the shoulders, first and foremost, of the "K.R.'s" and in a lesser degree of the shpana — the latter only in quite recent times.

But is it solely due to the sympathy of foreign Socialists, and a certain degree of conciliatoriness on the part of the Soviet Government, that the "politicals and party men" have been able to secure themselves a more or less bearable existence in the Solovky? Certainly not. It is in a large degree the achievement of the politicals themselves.

I am a convinced opponent of the politicals' social programme, the ultimate aspirations of which are indistinguishable from those of the Bolshevist programme and are absolutely Utopian. But none the less, I will pay due tribute to the persistency and fearlessness they have shown in upholding, if need be at personal sacrifice, the claims put forward by them as a corporate body in order to alleviate the detestable conditions of their life as exiles.

The discipline among the Socialists in the Solovky excels even that of the shpana. They will face a hunger strike, a rebellion, even death itself almost without hesitation, to attain the object they have set before them.

In the winter of 1923 the politicals at the Solovetsky Monastery, then over a thousand strong, made a skating rink near one of the caves. The camp administration observed parties of skaters on the rink singing revolutionary songs. They were ordered to stop singing, but did not obey. Then Nogteff brought a platoon of Red soldiers down to the rink and opened fire on the skaters without warning. Nine of them (six men and three women) were killed and many wounded.

The politicals declared a hunger strike and demanded that a commission of inquiry should be sent from Moscow. The whole body of them took part in the strike, on Popoff Island as well as on Solovetsky Island. Some of them could not stand upright from exhaustion, and were taken to hospital. One of these was the well-known "S.R." Bogdanoff, who until he was transferred to the Narym region in April, 1925, was generally recognised as the leader of the "politicals and party men" in the Solovky.

Nogteff went to the hospital to persuade them to stop the hunger strike. He was received with cries of "Executioner!" Bogdanoff, anxious that Nogteff should not worry the other sick men by his presence in the room, told the attendants to carry him out into the yard on a stretcher. Then he asked Nogteff:

"What can I do for you?"

Nogteff began again to try to persuade him to stop the hunger strike.

"Is that all you have to say?" Bogdanoff replied. "Take me back into hospital. I don't want to talk to a murderer."

The end of it was that the politicals had their way. In September of the same year a commission, consisting of Smirnoff (public prosecutor of the Supreme Court of the U.S.S.R.), Katanian (public prosecutor of the Gpu), and Soltz, was appointed. But the Socialists did not get from the commission what they expected. Nogteff was not punished in any way for shooting the nine persons. The commission found that he had acted in self-defence!

In the summer of 1924 the politicals again declared a hunger strike. This time they demanded that the food should be improved. The hunger strike lasted thirteen days. Several persons died, and about a hundred were taken to hospital. Moscow was appealed to, and this time granted the politicals' demand. From that time onward they began to receive daily 2 lbs. of bread (white and black), 1 lb. of meat, good butter, milk, eggs, etc., and these rations are still being issued to them at the time of writing.

At the end of 1924 and the beginning of 1925 students expelled from the universities began to arrive in the Solovky from Petrograd, Moscow and other towns. The Soviet Government had begun to expel and arrest students of bourgeois origin in order to make room for Communists.[30]

They came in three parties. The first two parties, consisting of about a hundred persons, including thirty women students, arrived at Kem in August, 1924. They included representatives of all parties (Monarchists, "S.R.'s," "S.D.'s," Anarchists, etc.). They declared that they were prisoners of the "political and party" category and demanded that they should be quartered in caves, with the privileges of the other cave dwellers, and receive the increased ration. The administration refused their request. The students declared a hunger strike with the friendly support of all the politicals. After several persons had died of starvation the students were recognised as political prisoners and sent to live in caves on Kond Island.

Kond Island lies about ten miles from the monastery. Formerly "seksoty" (secret Gpu agents) of both sexes used to be sent there; it is their business to promote espionage and paid delation among the prisoners. Nogteff bribes useful people by giving them better rations, gets everything

30   cf. "The Tcheka," by George Popoff, pp. 257-259.

he wants out of them, and when they are no longer required, quarters them in remote caves.

The third party of students (twenty-six in number, including two Anarchists) arrived at Kem in April, 1925. On the journey from Petrograd to Kem they smashed up the trucks in which they were travelling. Their demand to be treated as politicals was refused by the administration. The students, again supported by the politicals, declared a hunger strike, which lasted five weeks. Nogteff appealed to the Gpu, which ordered him to send the students back to Petrograd. I do not know what happened to them afterwards.

The "politicals and party men" carry on all negotiations with the authorities through "General" Eichmans, as they object to having any communication with Nogteff. They dare even to boycott publicly the most exalted representatives of the Gpu and the "Narkomyust" (People's Commissariat for Justice).

At the end of 1924 a so-called "unloading commission," consisting of Smirnoff, Katanian, Gleb Boky and a secretary, came to the Solovky. The prisoners hoped much from it, but their hopes were not realised. The commission certainly unloaded the Solovky, but only as regards shpana; nearly four hundred ordinary criminals were released, but not a single "K.R." or political.

When bidding farewell to the departing shpana, Katanian announced to the assembled prisoners:

"If the prisoners who are being released now reform and become useful citizens of the Soviet Republic, I shall come back next year and liberate another batch."

Thus the fate of the "K.R.'s" and politicals was made dependent on the conduct of ordinary criminals when set at liberty!

The commission stayed in the Solovky three days, and spent most of their time out shooting. The Tchekists exterminated the last survivors of the wild and tame animals, the latter introduced by the monks at some earlier period. On the last day Katanian visited the caves on Solovetsky Island, but the politicals drove him away with cries of "Go away, murderer! To hell with the executioner!"

The public prosecutor of the Supreme Court, Smirnoff, called a meeting and made a long speech. His speech was entirely devoted to controverting "the impudent calumnies of the émigré White Guard Press and foreign bourgeois newspapers." He attacked in particular the émigré Socialist paper Dni[31] for "misleading the proletariat of Europe by its criminal falsehoods about the Solovky."

On his return to Moscow he wrote and published a pamphlet entitled "The Solovky" (State Printing Office, Moscow, 1925), in which he stated that "complete liberty" prevailed there, that the food was "excellent," and that the treatment of the prisoners by the administration was "more than lenient."

To crown the whole performance, Smirnoff did not shrink from open mockery of the prisoners. A large number of copies of the pamphlet were sent to the Solovetsky camps and distributed to us — to us, who were tasting every minute of every day the "liberty," the "excellent food" and "more than lenient" treatment by the administration of which Smirnoff talked!

If Nogteff, Eichmans and their fellows listen to what the politicals have to say, the attitude of the lower personnel can be taken for granted. The conversations of the politicals with the commanders of the labour regiments and companies, quartermasters, and overseers of the kitchens and workshops have the tone of orders. Their headman Bogdanoff, when speaking to any subordinate in the commandant's office, always began his sentences with the words "we wish" instead of "we ask." Before rations were distributed, Bogdanoff used to go to the quartermaster and choose the best meat, white bread, and so on, for his section of the prisoners. His successor as headman, the Social Democrat Mamuloff, a lawyer from Vladikavkaz, enjoys the same rights.

The politicals, having plenty of time to themselves, are able to educate their children, and bring them up according to their own political views. One sees a ten-year-old boy, the son of a political, walking through the huts, greeting the Tchekists and sentries with abuse, and, when the prisoners ask him in fun to which party he belongs, replying proudly:

"I'm a Socialist. Down with the Communist usurpers!"

---

31   Published formerly in Berlin, now in Paris, and edited by Kerensky.

IX. THE WOMEN'S FATE

Horrible Companionship — How Card Losses are Paid — A Tchek-ist's Harem — "Rouble" and "Half-rouble" Women — Venereal Diseases.

But the greatest blessing the politicals enjoy is that their wives and children are not compelled to associate with the women of the shpana. The company of these women is horrible.

There are at present about six hundred women in the Solovetsky camps. At the monastery they are quartered in the "Women's Building" in the Kremlin; on Popoff Island they occupy the whole of hut No. 1 and portions of other huts. Three-quarters of them are the wives, mistresses, relatives or simply the accomplices of the common criminals.

Women are officially transported to the Solovky (and to the Narym region) for "persistent prostitution." At regular intervals, in all the large towns of European and Asiatic Russia, raids against prostitutes are carried out in order that they may be sent to the concentration camps. The prostitutes, who under the Soviet regime have combined to form regular professional unions, from time to time organise street processions in Moscow and Petrograd by way of protest against the raids and the transportations; but this is of little avail.

The character and ways of the female shpana are so savage that a description of them, to anyone unacquainted with life in the Solovetsky prison, may sound like the delusions of a madman.

For example, when they go to the bath-house, they undress a long time before in their huts and walk about stark naked, to the accompaniment of roars of laughter and approving remarks from the camp personnel.

The female criminals are just as addicted to gambling card games as the men. If they lose, they hardly ever have any money, decent clothes or food with which to pay. In consequence, the most barbarous scenes may be witnessed every day in the camps. The women play cards on the condition that the loser must immediately go to one of the men's huts and give herself to ten men one after the other. This must take place in the presence of regular witnesses. The camp administration has never intervened to put a stop to this loathsomeness.

The influence the female criminals have on educated women, "K.R."

prisoners, can be imagined. The foulest cursing, in which the names of God, Christ, the Virgin and all the saints are called upon, universal drunkenness, indescribable debauchery, thieving, filth, syphilis — all this must in the long run be too much for the most stubborn nature.

To send an honest woman to the Solovky is to turn her in a few months into something worse than a prostitute — a piece of dumb, dirty flesh, an object of barter, at the disposal first and foremost of the camp personnel itself.

Every Tchekist in the Solovky has from three to five concubines at the same time. Toropoff, who was appointed assistant to the Kem commandant on the administrative side in 1924, established a regular harem in the camp, continually replenished according to his choice and at his orders. The Red soldiers who guard the camp violate women unpunished.

According to the camp rules, twenty-five women — "K.R.'s" and shpana — are selected every day to act as servants to the Red divisions guarding the Solovky. The soldiers are so lazy that the prisoners even make their beds.

The headman of the Kem camp, Tchistakoff, not only has his dinner cooked and his boots cleaned by women, but they even have to wash him!

The youngest and prettiest women are usually chosen, and the Tchekists are free to treat them as they please.

All the women in the Solovky are officially divided into three categories: (1) a rouble woman (rublevaya), (2) a half-rouble woman (poltinitchnaya), and (3) a fifteen kopek woman (piatialtynnaya).

If one of the camp authorities requires a "first-class" woman, i.e., a young "K.R." who has not been long in the camp, he says to the sentry: "Bring me a rouble woman."

Honest women who refuse the "improved ration" which the Tchekists give their concubines very soon die of under-nourishment or tuberculosis. Such cases are particularly frequent on Solovetsky Island, where the bread usually does not last through the winter — i.e., till navigation begins and fresh supplies can be brought — and the already miserable rations are cut down by a half.

The Tchekists and the shpana infect the women with syphilis and other venereal diseases. How widespread these diseases are in the Solovky may be judged from this fact. Until recently the syphilitics, both male and female, were quartered on Popoff Island, in a special hut (No. 8). But their number increased to such an extent in the few months before I escaped that hut No. 8 would not hold them all, and the administration could think of no better solution of the problem than to put the patients in other huts, occupied by uninfected persons. Of course, this only led to a still more rapid increase in the number of cases.

If their solicitations meet with resistance, the Tchekists do not shrink from heaping insult on their victims. I will mention two out of a number of such cases known to me.

At the end of 1924 a very pretty Polish girl of seventeen was brought to the Solovky. She had been sentenced to be shot, along with her father and mother, for "espionage in the interests of Poland." The parents were shot, but as the girl was under age, the supreme penalty was in her case commuted to transportation to the Solovky for ten years.

The girl had the misfortune to attract Toropoff, but had the pluck to refuse his disgusting proposals. Thereupon Toropoff ordered her to be brought to the commandant's office, accused her of concealing "counter-revolutionary" documents on her person, stripped her naked and searched her under the eyes of the whole camp guard — examining with care those parts of her body where it seemed to him that the "documents" might best be concealed.

One day in February, 1925, a Tchekist named Popoff appeared in the women's hut very drunk, accompanied by a number of other Tchekists, also drunk. He went up to Madame X's bed. This lady belonged to the highest social circles and had been sent to the Solovky for ten years after her husband had been shot. Popoff dragged her out of bed and said:

"Won't you come outside the wire with us?" (It was there that women were violated.)

Madame X was in a state of raving hysteria till the next morning.

Uneducated and half-educated "K.R." women are exploited by the Tchekists without scruple. Particularly lamentable is the fate of the many Cossack women, whose husbands, fathers and brothers have been shot and they themselves transported.

X. FOREIGN PRISONERS

Espionage for Mexico! — A Cryptic Message — Gpu Tactics — Attempts to Escape Savagely Punished.

Most of the foreigners in the Solovky were sent there on the charge of "espionage for the benefit of the international bourgeoisie" (Clause 66). Sometimes a second clause is brought into action as well as Clause 66, quite groundlessly; the Tchekist "jurisprudence" is most skilful in discovering a crime where there is not the shadow of one.

Among the prisoners in the Solovky are Count Villa, Mexican Consul-General in Egypt, and his wife. It must have been, one would think, rather difficult for a man living in Cairo to direct "Mexican espionage" in Soviet Russia, especially in view of the fact that the Consul-General does not speak or understand a single word of Russian. The circumstances of his arrest were as follows.

Count Villa's wife is a Georgian lady, née Princess Karalova. In 1924 she and her husband came to the Caucasus to visit her mother, with the permission of the Soviet Government and with their passports in order. Unluckily, just at that time the Georgian rebellion broke out. The Bolsheviks shot the Countess's brother, Prince Karaloff, and sent the diplomatist and his wife to the Solovky for three years for "espionage for the benefit of Mexico." They arrived there in February, 1925.

The Consul-General is living in the Solovky by virtue of a diplomatic passport guaranteeing him personal immunity! On his arrival in the camp he tried to send to Mexico a full account of the outrage committed on him by the Soviet authorities, but the Solovetsky censorship destroyed it. Then the Count had recourse to the language of Æsop and sent his Government a telegram which began with the words:

"I am making a very interesting tour in the north of Russia."

Evidently the fact of the Mexican diplomatist's transportation to the Solovky is known abroad, for not long before I escaped some things were sent to him from London by aeroplane (he had been robbed by the Tchekists when he was arrested). He carries on an active correspondence with Tchitcherin in French, demanding his release. But Mexico is a long way off; she has no merchant fleet or money to lend the Soviets; and so the Commissariat for Foreign Affairs, in its polite replies to its colleague's letters, passes over in silence the question of his liberation. The only result of Tchitcherin's letters was that the Consul-General was exempted from work in the camp. But Countess Villa, like all women "K.R.'s," scrubs hut floors and washes Tchekists' shirts.

Representatives of every nation, great as well as small, may be met with in the Solovky — Englishmen, Italians, Japanese, Frenchmen and Germans, besides natives of lesser States. The reasons for their transportation are as a rule shamelessly inadequate. Is seems as if the Gpu were deliberately frightening foreigners away, so that they shall not visit Russia, become acquainted with the country or open commercial or any other kind of relations with it. I referred in an earlier chapter to the case of the Hungarian manufacturer Frenckell, whom the Vneshtorg (Foreign Trade Office) invited to Russia and then sent to the Solovky. There have been many cases of the kind. For example, an Estonian named Motise went to Moscow to see the All-Russian Exhibition, and was sent straight from the Exhibition to the Solovky!

At a time when there was a Government crisis in Lithuania, and the struggle between the political parties had reached an abnormal degree of bitterness, a member of the defeated party fled from the country into Soviet Russia. He was an engineer officer in the Lithuanian army. He was completely strange to Soviet Russia and to the Communists, and believed that he would find in the neighbouring country asylum as a political refugee. But directly he crossed the frontier he was arrested, accused, despite his protests, of "organising a counter-revolutionary plot and espionage in the interests of Lithuania," and sent to the Solovky!

In the monastery and on Popoff Island there are a large number of persons formerly attached to the diplomatic missions of foreign States. They are mostly Poles, Estonians, Finlanders, Latvians and Lithuanians, employees of the Legations, Consulates and missions of their respective countries, who have been arrested on the charge of "espionage" and, more rarely, "speculation."

All the foreigners live in the constant hope that their Governments will exchange them for Communists. The administration treats them cruelly. They get the same rations as the "K.R.'s," and the work they are given is for the most part severe.

There have lately been several attempts to escape. The would-be fugitives have mostly been Estonians, Latvians, Finlanders and Poles. Nogteff has, therefore, given orders that prisoners of those nationalities shall not be taken to work outside the camps.

Attempts to escape — always unsuccessful — are punished first by cruel torture and then by shooting (although, according to the regulations, the maximum punishment is the prolongation of the prisoner's term of imprisonment by one year).

In March, 1925, a Finlander attempted to escape from the Solovetsky Monastery. He had gone to the latrine, accompanied by a sentry, climbed over the wall and found himself on the seashore. In these latitudes spring generally comes late, and the ice by the Kremlin was still thick enough to bear. The Finlander fled as fast as he could towards the woods, a little way along the coast. He was observed; the alarm was given and shots were fired after him. Just as he had reached the woods, where he could have hidden until he could continue his flight with better prospects of escaping recapture, he came unexpectedly to a break in the ice, and halted in indecision. The Tchekists caught him.

The Finlander was brought back to the camp. He was beaten for nearly an hour with such violence that the thick "Smolensky sticks" were broken. Then, all dripping with blood, he was shot.

XI. A "CHANGE OF CABINET"

Kem Camp's New Rulers — A Military Parade — A Much-Married Tchekist — Old Abuses Continued.

In the spring of 1924 the personnel of the concentration camp on Popoff Island was changed. The members of the Uslon (Direction of the Northern Camps for Special Purposes) and, at the monastery itself, all the Tchekists remained at their posts. This was what the prisoners called the "change of cabinet."

A Moscow Tchekist, Ivan Ivanovitch Kirilovsky, formerly a sergeant in one of the Guards regiments, was appointed commandant of the Kem camp in place of Gladkoff. As stated in an earlier chapter, he refused to take over until a commission was appointed by the central Government to examine the camp accounts. When the commission discovered that gross extravagance and fraud had taken place, Gladkoff was sentenced to transportation for five years for "peculation and a negligent attitude towards his exalted (?) duties." Mamonoff, who was directly responsible for the frauds, was not punished at all; and, for that matter, Gladkoff himself was pardoned two days after his sentence and given a new appointment in the Gpu at Kaluga.

Before Kirilovsky's arrival it was said in the camps that he was a decent fellow. We were soon to have ocular demonstration of his "decency." Kirilovsky is still in command of the camp, with the same assistants.

His arrival was the occasion for an elaborate ceremony. Eichmans, already familiar to the reader, whose dream was to turn the camps into military colonies of the Araktcheeff[32] epoch, paraded the starving prisoners, including women and children, several days in succession, and made them execute movements, obey words of command, and so on, in military style. When Kirilovsky approached the camp, we were drawn up in two ranks.

"Attention! . . . Right dress!"

The headman went up to Kirilovsky with his report.

"All correct in the labour regiment under my command."

---

32   Count Araktcheeff (1769-1834), the great Roman military organiser. The military colonies scheme, which he endeavoured (unsuccessfully) to carry out, was one of the many projects of the Emperor Alexander I.

The commanders of all the labour companies did the same. Then Kirilovsky greeted us:

"Good day!"

"Good —— day!"

This cruel farce went on for nearly an hour. At last Kirilovsky asked whether anyone had any request to make, or any complaint against the administration. His question, of course, remained unanswered. If anyone had had the audacity to make a complaint, he would have been taken to the "Sekirka" (the place of punishment) that very day and been flogged to death with "Smolensky sticks."

Kirilovsky's assistant on the administrative side was, as I have mentioned, Toropoff, a typical vagabond, with goggling sheep's eyes. He was formerly a platoon commander in the 95th Division of Gpu troops, which does guard duties on Popoff Island. Apart from his devastating stupidity, his principal characteristic is that he gets married everywhere he goes. On Popoff Island he was not content with a harem of women prisoners, and got married — for the sixth time — to a "cod-eater." ("Cod-eaters" is the name given by the prisoners to the inhabitants of the fishing settlements round the camps, whose main article of food is cod.)

Kirilovsky's assistant on the economic side was one Nikolai Nikolaevitch Popoff. He was always extremely well dressed, was not a Tchekist and not even a Communist. He was a most enigmatic personality. Sometimes he said he had been an officer in the Guards, sometimes an official with special duties in one of the Tsarist Ministries, sometimes Trotsky's adjutant. He was, in any case, a man of very good education and outward polish. He had an impediment in his speech, and was malignant and cruel in his dealings with "K.R.'s." When the prisoners passed him on their way to work, Popoff used to say to his suite of Tchekists — in a loud voice, so that the "K.R.'s" might hear:

"There's a pack of criminals — do you hear? — criminals! They're our enemies. We'll put the wind up the whole crowd of them!"

The "change of cabinet" made little difference to the situation of the prisoners. The only modification was that "putting the wind up" them, and the thieving of State funds and their modest rations by the administration, became more constant than before. Gladkoff stole openly, Kirilovsky under a camouflage of "honesty."

The Solovetsky life and regime in general — the heavy toll of labour, the reprisals, the self-indulgent manner of living of the personnel — remained as they had been.

XII. DAILY LIFE, WORK AND FOOD

"A Place in the Lamp-light" — "Outside" and "Inside" Work — No Exemption for Illness — Horrors of Wood-cutting — How We were Fed — Prisoners Starved and Government Cheated.

The huts in Popoff Island camp are about forty yards long and ten yards in breadth. The politicals' hut is twice as large as the others. From two hundred to three hundred persons are as a rule quartered in each hut; in Nos. 5 and 6, occupied mainly by shpana, there are over seven hundred persons.

One cannot breathe as night approaches; the stench is awful. In the evening, when the prisoners return from work, the huts, full of cracks, holes in the roofs, and draughts from all quarters, are so cold that the inmates shiver like men with fever. It is impossible to sleep at night for the stuffiness and human exhalations. We used to strip naked and pile all our clothes on top of us.

The board-beds are arranged along the walls in two tiers. Everyone tries to get an "upper berth," for if you lie below a continual shower of lice, remains of food and spittle descends on you. Sanguinary fights take place for beds in the upper tier.

The electric power station was not constructed till the end of 1924. Until then an apology for a lamp — a tin containing a wick slightly damped with paraffin — flickered in the middle of each hut. This gave light to the three or four beds nearest to it; all the rest of the hut was in darkness. Now every hut is lighted with a small electric light globe (16 watts), but this is quite inadequate for such large huts. There is always a crowd under the one tiny lamp, trying to read, or write to their relations. The absence of light is particularly trying in winter. The headmen of the huts profit by the situation to take bribes, either in money or in kind, for "a place in the lamp-light"!

"Nep" — the New Economic Policy — affected even the Solovky. They were placed on a "self-supporting" basis, and the sum granted annually by the central Government for the upkeep of the camps was considerably reduced. Thus in the present year (1925) the Solovky received only 250,000 gold roubles as against two millions demanded by Boky and Nogteff.

There is no need to feed the prisoners, even on a semi-starvation diet. But it is quite indispensable that the administration should pocket large sums of money. Therefore the Natchuslon and his minions have crushed the last drops of energy out of the prisoners and turned them all into dumb slaves.

Work in the Solovky is divided into two categories — "outside" (outside the wire fence) and "inside" (inside the camp). For outside work the prisoners are generally taken from Solovetsky and Popoff Islands to the mainland. Among the tasks which come under the head of outside work are: fetching wood, draining the marshes, laying, clearing and keeping in order railway lines and roads (earth and wooden), cutting timber for the necessities of the camp and for export, and loading and unloading timber, stones and supplies. The names of the vessels used for transporting cargo are the steamers Gleb Boky and Neva and the barge Klara, so named in honour of the German woman Communist Clara Zetkin.

By inside work is meant clearing away snow, helping in the kitchen and workshops, removing refuse from the latrines and the huts occupied by ordinary criminals, and performing services for the Tchekists. The women scrub the floors of the huts and offices, cook food, do the Tchekists' and Red soldiers' washing, sewing, etc.

Work begins at 6 a.m. both summer and winter. According to the regulations work stops at 7 p.m., but in the Solovky there is a twelve hours' working day, with an interval for dinner at 1 p.m. Actually work goes on much longer than this, at the discretion of the supervising Tchekist. This is particularly the case in summer, when the prisoners literally have to work to fainting point; in that season work often goes on from 6 a.m. to 12 or 1 the following night.

There is no Sunday in the Solovky, nor is there any other day of rest in the week. Every day is a working day. On the great festivals, Easter, Christmas, etc., the hours of work are usually lengthened in order to insult the feelings of the religious prisoners.[33] Only one day in the year is set apart as a festival . . . the First of May.

Illness, physical weakness, old age and extreme youth are not taken into account in the slightest degree. A refusal to work on the ground of illness, even when the illness is obvious to the Tchekists themselves, involves, for a first offence, removal to the "Sekirka" (the place of punishment), and, for a second offence, shooting, although, according to law, the punishment for refusal to work — and even then only without adequate cause — is the extension of the term of imprisonment by one year.

33   cf. p. 99.

The most exhausting labour is fetching wood in winter. This work is absolutely insupportable. You stand up to your knees in snow, so that it is difficult to move. Huge tree-trunks, cut away with axes, fall on the prisoners, sometimes killing them on the spot. Clad in rags, with no mittens, with only bast shoes on your feet, hardly able to stand for weakness caused by under-nourishment, your hands and whole body are frozen stiff in the bitter cold.

The minimum daily task is as follows: four men have to cut, split and pile four cubic sajenes (a sajene is about two yards), and till they have done this they are not allowed to return to the camp. An extra hardship attached to all outside work is that if the prisoners do not get through their minimum task up to time and return to camp punctually, the shpana take the kitchen by storm, and they get no dinner.

Once I was sent to the shore near Kem to cut wood with a party of other "K.R.'s." The wood was urgently needed, and we were chased out of our huts at 5 a.m. As a rule sentries are changed at 12 p.m. But this time, for some reason or other, no relief for our escort was sent to the wood where we were at work. The Red soldiers, not remarkable for discipline, took us back to the camp, demanding to be relieved. Toropoff cursed them and called up a fresh escort of Tchekists. Then we were driven straight back to our work in the same wood without any interval for dinner, and did not return till 4 a.m. In other words, we worked for nineteen hours in severe cold without food, and without interruption save for our two extra marches to and from the camp!

Everything in the Solovky that could be plundered was plundered long ago, and everything that could be sold was sold. To obtain new resources, the authorities made various big labour contracts in the territory of the "autonomous" Karelian Republic — for example, for the construction of a road from Kem to Ukhta. But seeing that unemployment menaces Karelia itself, the Karelian Vtsik continually complained to Moscow that the Slon was taking the bread out of the mouths of the Karelians. The agreements were cancelled, but the Solovetsky administration profited by them nevertheless. This is what happened. Nogteff submitted to Moscow more or less fantastic schemes for labour undertakings on Karelian territory, and asked the Gpu for a money subsidy and spirits, the latter for the workmen, toiling chin-deep in the marshes! The money and spirits, when they arrived, were divided among the Tchekists, those most intimate with Nogteff receiving the larger share.

As constructional and commercial schemes did not yield a large enough profit, the Solovetsky authorities saw the only way out in a reduction of the rations. This they proceeded to carry out.

Every prisoner, however hard the labour he was engaged on, was henceforward given 1 lb. of black bread daily. The bread is issued for ten days ahead, so that at the end of this time it is as hard as a stone. The bread is badly baked; the flour is stale and has a bitter taste.

Hot food is issued twice a day. Dinner is a plate of soup, made of mouldy codfish — evil-smelling water, without groats or butter; supper a tureen of millet or buckwheat gruel, again without butter. The "K.R.'s" often get no supper, because the shpana prisoners, who have lost their own portion at cards, go and rob the kitchen.

In the camp accounts every prisoner is entered as receiving 3 zolotniks of sugar a day, or (as this also is issued for ten days in advance) 30 zolotniks per issue. (A zolotnik is 1/96 of a Russian lb.) What each prisoner actually gets every ten days is a half-glass of half-frozen liquefied sugar containing 10 or 12 zolotniks. The Tchekists mix the sugar with water and thus steal 18 to 20 zolotniks on each ration, which, in a camp containing several thousand prisoners, means a profit of two or three score poods every day of issue.

It is also stated in the accounts that the prisoners receive one-eighth of a lb. of butter and one-eighth of a lb. of tobacco. In reality no butter or tobacco at all are issued in the camps. Casks of butter and hundreds of poods of tobacco are sold at Kem by the authorities, who pocket the money.

Lastly, according to the regulations, every prisoner engaged in hard bodily labour is supposed to receive, besides his food ration, 35 kopeks a day pocket money. The money for this purpose is sent by the central Government and is additional to the ordinary budget. No prisoner has ever received these 35 kopeks. Every penny of this "bonus" goes into the pockets of the Tchekists.

It is possible that before the "change of cabinet" the feeding in the Solovky was better than it is now. Then the prisoners got preserves, large quantities of which — enough for two years — were left behind by the British. The present ration amounts to nothing else than the murder of the prisoners by a slow death from starvation. I calculate, on the basis of the requirements of a man engaged in hard bodily labour, that this ration, issued for ten days, is barely sufficient for two or three days!

As I mentioned earlier in my narrative, the politicals receive the "improved ration," which is almost sufficient.

The Red soldiers get the "northern ration," with plenty of butter, fats, white bread, and even spirits.

XIII. HOSPITAL HORRORS

Hospitals Without Drugs — "Prisoners Must Not be Ill" — A Mad-woman in Command — Mortality among Prisoners Encouraged — A Kindly Tchekist.

The "Medpomoshtsh"[34] (medical help) in the Solovetsky Islands is in fact medical helplessness. Owing partly to lack of resources, partly to the ill-will of the administration of the camps and the secret instructions of the Moscow Gpu, there is in the Solovky only one really effective cure for illness — death.

The sanitary conditions in the camps are horrible. Not only are huts, kitchens, latrines, etc., in an incredible state of filth, but the Solovetsky "hospitals" themselves can truthfully be called breeding-places for epidemics. The damp, marshy locality, the bad water, and the millions of mosquitoes and lice all render powerful assistance in creating and spreading disease.

The prisoners have no change of linen, no soap, no proper clothes or boots. Their organisms, debilitated by permanent under-nourishment and hard work, are not in a state to resist disease.

There is a "hospital" in the Kremlin of the Solovetsky Monastery. The word should be placed within quotation marks, because this hospital has no drugs of any kind, the beds are indescribably dirty, the patients are given the ordinary starvation ration, and the place is very often unheated.

The doctor in charge of it, himself a prisoner, has repeatedly attempted to persuade the Natchuslon that in the absence of drugs, bed linen (the patients lie on bare boards), soap, eatable food, and a latrine in the hospital itself (the patients have to go out in the yard in all temperatures, even in winter), the "treatment" of the prisoners is nothing else than deliber-ate murder. But the Solovetsky administration has always refused his demands. Fresh thousands arrive in the Solovky every year, and the huts must be cleared of "superfluous elements." Once Nogteff actually said:

"Prisoners have no business to be ill!"

The "hospital" on Popoff Island may serve as another fairly good specimen of Solovetsky "medical help." A woman is in charge of it, by

34   Meditsinskaya pomoshtsh.

name Lvova (Maria Nikolaevna). She is a highly-trained doctor. Before she was sent into exile she was in the Red Cross, and served on literally every front in the Great War and the civil war. Subsequently she was a "seksotka" (secret woman agent for the Gpu) but was ascertained to have "talked indiscreetly about secret Gpu affairs," and was sent to the Solovky for five years.

This woman, perhaps not bad in the depths of her heart, has been shattered by her work for the Gpu and the life in the Solovky. She has lost all self-control. No one in the Solovky, even the most disreputable common criminals, curses with such complete mastery of the art, applies such foul terms of abuse to men and God Himself, as the directress of the hospital. Criminals often go to the hospital just to listen to Lvova's swearing and introduce her latest gems of obscenity into their own talk.

No one in the Solovky drinks so much, or drinks him- or herself into such a swinish condition, as Maria Nikolaevna. She has reached the lowest pitch of moral disintegration. And her care of the sick is what might be expected of a person in such a state. Human life, for her, has ceased to have the slightest value. The hospitals of the Solovetsky Islands are in themselves almost a guarantee that the patients who enter them will die en masse. Lvova accelerates the patient's death by her roughness, her complete indifference to their sufferings, the cruelty of a person on the verge of insanity. When patients complain of the horrible state of things in her hospital, she always replies:

"The worse the better; all the more of you'll kick the bucket" — followed by a quite unprintable oath.

But I will not raise my hand to throw a stone at this woman; from living in insane conditions she herself has become insane. But have Nogteff and the other "administrators" of the Solovetsky Islands neither eyes nor ears? Why have they put a madwoman at the head of the medical service on Popoff Island?

I gave the answer to this question at the beginning of the chapter. The central authorities of the Gpu, and under them the Solovetsky Tchekists, are deliberately increasing the mortality in the Solovky. A further proof of this is in the fact that prisoners are not allowed to send for a doctor from Kem even at their own expense. The Kem doctor attends only the Solovetsky Tchekists.

The "K.R.'s" and politicals fear the Solovetsky hospitals like the plague. If prisoners of these categories fall ill, and cannot cure themselves by "home remedies," they die in the huts, begging not to be taken to hospital. Only the shpana, who, like Lvova, set no value either on their own lives or other people's, go to hospital of their own accord. In consequence, the ordinary criminals die in dozens daily, mainly of scurvy.

The water of the Solovetsky Islands has in it some quality which ruins the teeth, and the consequent toothache is intensified by cold and the draughts in the huts. A dentist is urgently needed in the camps. It is true that there is a dentist in the Kremlin of the Solovetsky Monastery — Malivanoff, known to the reader as an A.R.A. worker, punished by the Bolsheviks in return for his services — but he has no drugs or instruments.

On Popoff Island this question is decided in a radical manner. There is a man named Brusilovsky in the camp. Before the Revolution he was a feldsher, or local surgeon; after the Revolution — a Tchekist belonging to the Gpu of Elisavetgrad, in what is now the Government of Odessa, formerly the Government of Kherson. He was sent to the Solovky under Clause 76 of the Criminal Code — "armed banditism." Despite his profession of Tchekist, Brusilovsky is a very nice, sympathetic fellow. He decided to do what he could for the victims of toothache, and somehow got hold of an ordinary blacksmith's pincers, with which he pulls out teeth.

Of course, nothing can be done to cure the teeth while they are decaying, for there is nothing to do it with, neither drugs nor instruments; all that can be done is to pull them out, to which the sufferers always readily consent. Brusilovsky never takes any money for his services. He has a huge practice, especially among the shpana, whose teeth he pulls out rows at a time. The first time he pulled out quite sound teeth too, for practice.

This compassionate Tchekist treats syphilis too. His method of dealing with this complaint is also the last word in Solovetsky science. A compound of infusions of herbs, spirit and something else is injected with an ordinary syringe. He evidently still needs practice in this branch, for syphilis is on the increase in the camps, and the mortality from it is growing steadily.

XIV. HOW "USEFUL CITIZENS" ARE MADE

Chief Punishments — A Freezing Dungeon — "To the Mosquitoes!"
— A Mediæval Torture — Mass Shootings No Longer Necessary.

The leaders of the Communist Party declare that the Northern Camps for Special Purposes are something in the nature of a reformatory. The punishments administered in these establishments, they would have the world believe, are intended to make the prisoners mend their ways and become useful citizens of the Soviet Republic.

In reality, the camp punishments, like the camp medical arrangements, are based upon no other calculation than that of sending the largest possible number of prisoners, more or less swiftly, to "the other side."

Refusal to work, insubordination towards the authorities, "counter-revolutionary propaganda," insulting words or behaviour to the personnel, the discovery of a "criminal past" (this is Vasko's occupation), attempted escape — for these offences there are a number of punishments, in accordance with the heinousness of the offence. I will mention the chief punishments:

(1) The "Sekirka."
(2) "To the Mosquitoes!"
(3) Prolongation of the term of imprisonment.
(4) "Stone sacks."
(5) Shooting.

Such corrective measures as blows in the face, the confiscation of parcels from relations for an indefinite time (for the benefit of the confiscator!), flogging with the whip or only "Smolensky sticks" without "stone sacks," etc., are so common in the Solovky that there is no need to dwell on them.

The "Sekirka" is a prison on the notorious Sekirova hill, on Solovetsky Island, two miles from the Kremlin. In bygone days it was the cave of one of the most honoured of the legendary heroes of the Solovetsky Islands. The "guilty" prisoner is sent to the Sekirka for a term of from two to six months. The regime there is as follows. The prisoner receives daily half a pound of bread, a jug of cold water, and nothing else. All the doors and windows of the cave are fastened. He has no communication at all with the outside world. The dungeon is absolutely unheated. As a rule, when the term of his punishment comes to an end, there is nothing left of the prisoner but a frozen corpse. In rare cases a half-dead skeleton emerges from the Sekirka.

"To the Mosquitoes!" is a form of punishment very popular with the Solovetsky Tchekists. The manner of its infliction is as follows. The prisoner is stripped naked and made to stand on a particular stone opposite the commandant's office. He is ordered, with threats of "stone sacks" and shooting, to stand absolutely still, not to move a finger and not to drive away the mosquitoes, which cover the poor wretch's body as with a thick black crust. The torture is continued for several hours. When the punishment is over, the victim's body is one huge sore from the bites of the poisonous insects. The weaker prisoners die, and the stronger cannot sit or lie down for many weeks after the punishment.

Prolongation of the term of imprisonment is a punishment now comparatively seldom applied, for the simple reason that the orders recently circulated by the Gpu have made every prisoner a convict for an indefinite term. When he has served his two, three, five or ten years, he is sent on from the Solovky to the Petchersk region, then to the Narym, then to the Zyriansk, and so on, unendingly. For more serious "offences," therefore, the Tchekists send the prisoners to the "sacks."

In the old times, every monk in the Kremlin, and every holy man in the caves, had a small cellar cut in the rock near his cell, in which he kept his food supplies. These cellars, three or four feet in depth, have no doors, and the food was placed in them from above through small openings.

These are the famous "stone sacks." The Tchekists take the prisoner to the "sack," and ask him:

"How'll you get in — head first or feet first?"

If the prisoner gets into the "sack" head first, he is beaten with "Smolensky sticks" on the back and legs; if he gets in feet first, he is beaten about the head and face. The beating goes on till his whole body is inside the "sack." The "sack" is too narrow for him to sit, and too low for him to stand up straight, so that he is obliged to stand with his knees bent and his head poked forward. He is imprisoned in the "sack" for a period varying between three days and a week. The rations are the same as at the Sekirka. Few people can endure this mediæval punishment.

There are no mass shootings at the Solovky like those carried out at the "White House," but individual shootings are very frequent, and are regarded as an ordinary occurrence. A larger or smaller number of prisoners are shot whenever the Soviet Government retaliates for measures of suppression against Communists in foreign States by a terrorist outburst on its own part. Thus, over a hundred persons, both Russians and foreigners, were shot after the suppression of the Communist revolt of December 1st, 1924, by the Estonian Government, and a rather smaller number after the suppression of the rebellion in Bulgaria.

I gathered from the candid statements of the Tchekists that the Gpu has now no need to make a regular practice of mass shootings, because more humane measures — slow murder from starvation, work beyond the prisoners' strength, and "medical help" — are perfectly adequate substitutes.

It would be a mistake to suppose that one must commit some kind of offence to be sent to the Sekirka, the "sacks" and the mosquitoes, or to be shot. The prisoners are handed over by the central authorities to the unchecked caprice of the camp administration. If the Tchekists dislike your face, if you are seen crossing yourself on the sly, if you have said anything about your hard lot in your letters to your relations — the Sekirka and the "sacks" open their dreadful doors to you.

XV. HOW THE TCHEKISTS LIVE

Luxurious Proletarians — Merry Gatherings at Kem — A Revolting Orgy — "Holding the Banner of Communism Aloft" — How Criminals are Released.

The concentration camp on Solovetsky Island is guarded by the 3rd Escort Regiment of the Gpu troops (300 rifles strong), and that on Popoff Island by the 95th Division of the Gpu troops (150 strong). In spite of the good food they receive, scurvy rages among the Red soldiers, as does also syphilis. The soldiers, with the exception of those on duty guarding the camps, live in private quarters.

The Solovky guards, drawn from the criminal canaille which, after the October Revolution, suddenly discovered its "class consciousness" and joined the Communist Party in tens of thousands, spend all their time in card-playing, debauchery, swilling home-distilled spirits and drunken orgies.

In this they follow the example of the higher officials. The life led by the Solovky authorities is far from proletarian. Nogteff, Eichmans, Vasko, Kirilovsky, Popoff and the rest deny themselves nothing. Having earned piles of money at the expense of the prisoners, the "administrators" lead a thoroughly non-Communistic life. Liquor, clothes, and other things are always arriving for them in truck-loads from Moscow, Petrograd and Kem. I myself took part in the unloading of two of these trucks. They contained different kinds of vodka, Russian and foreign wines, including champagne, liqueurs, all kinds of hors d'œuvres, expensive clothes, both men's and women's — the latter for the harems — comfortable furniture, and so on.

The "administrators" are notorious for their orgies not only in the Solovky, but much further afield — all over Northern Russia. The scene of the debauches is usually Kem, where the Tchekists from the monastery and from Popoff Island assemble to make merry.

On Popoff Island itself they take place in the quarters of Kirilovsky, the commandant of the "Kemperraspredpunkt," who not long ago had the reputation of being a decently conducted man. They nearly always end in brawls.

For example, in August, 1924, a drinking-bout of the usual kind was held in Kirilovsky's quarters. Guests and host drank so heavily that

Kirilovsky felt ill, and they took him out into the fresh air. When he returned to the house, the guests, as drunk as pigs, were vomiting over the table, and his wife was lying on a sofa in Popoff's arms in a shameless posture.

Infuriated, Kirilovsky dragged Popoff from the sofa and flung him away so violently that his head went through the door. Popoff, however, managed to give him a blow in the face, smashing his glasses. Shots were fired. Popoff was dragged out of Kirilovsky's quarters and taken home, where he broke all the windows with his fists and, shedding bitter tears, began to bellow so that all the camp could hear him:

"They've killed me! They've killed me!"

It would appear that such a manner of life is ideal Communism, for in November, 1924, at the time of the anniversary of the October Revolution, the Natchuslon received a letter of thanks from the Moscow Gpu, in which the latter expressed its gratitude to Nogteff and his colleagues for "holding the banner of Communism aloft."

In the time which their alcoholic occupations leave at their disposal, the "administrators" of the Solovetsky Islands amuse themselves by amnestying prisoners of the shpana category. Every day, after navigation has begun, some five hundred prisoners are released.

The procedure is as follows. The ordinary criminals, male and female, are stripped of their last rags ("State clothing"), are given railway tickets to the towns where they live, and a supply of bread in accordance with the length of their journey. Then they are put into freight trucks stark naked, and sent off to Kem station! Naturally half the shpana rob somebody to get clothes directly they arrive at Kem station, and return to the camp to undergo an extra year's imprisonment. The rest go away naked.

None of the "K.R.'s" are ever liberated. From time to time it is rumoured that the politicals are to be released or transferred to a prison on the mainland of Russia. These rumours usually remain rumours; if politicals leave the Solovky it is only for another place of exile.

PART III OUR ESCAPE

I. THE ONLY WAY OUT

Bolshevist Hypocrisy — Prisoners for Life — The Student Nikolaeff's Escape — Failure of other Attempts.

The foreign workmen who come to Moscow in batches are given to understand by the Soviet Government that it, of course, is against the Solovky; it is willing to admit that the Solovky are a discredit to the "humane" rule of the workers and peasants. But, it asks, what is to be done? —— the counter-revolutionaries continue their struggle with the Soviet power, and so the Gpu insists on the maintenance of the concentration camps. The Gpu, for its part, puts the blame on the Council of People's Commissaries.

And while they are saying this, the Council of People's Commissaries and the Gpu are fettering their prisoners to the Solovky and its "continuations" for their whole lives — by sending them on to other more or less remote places. Since the autumn of 1924, by a special order of the Gpu — submitted to and confirmed by the Vtsik — every prisoner who has served his term in the Solovky is sent for three years to a "free settlement" in the Narym region, then to the Petchersk region for three years more, then to the Turukhansk and Zyriansk regions — that is to say, for twelve years in all. For those who somehow or other contrive not to die during these twelve years, a final reward is reserved — exile to a permanent settlement in Eastern Siberia.

Thus, whatever "offence" you have been found guilty of, however you have conducted yourself in the Solovky, you will never be released. Every person transported by the Soviet Government is doomed to die on his journeyings from prison to prison, from one place of forced exile to another.

The terrible knowledge that one is a convict for life, that, after the Solovky, one will be driven off to new torments, be given a new Nogteff, a new Kirilovsky, a new ration, be compelled to do more hard labour, get into other "sacks," rot in another Sekirka, makes the prisoner realise that this endless, hopeless pilgrimage of pain must be cut short once and for all — by escape.

But a successful escape from the Solovky is a miracle, a fabulous piece of good fortune, granted to a few out of scores of thousands.

During the time that I spent in the Solovky I heard of only one case in which a prisoner had escaped from the Solovky — and he did not escape abroad, but into the interior of Russia. He was a medical student named Nikolaeff — a "K.R." He succeeded by some means or other in getting himself employed as a clerk in the camp commandant's office, and winning the confidence of the Tchekists by pretended hatred of "K.R.'s." He came to manage the whole business of the camp, had all the forms and papers at his disposal, and occasionally even went to Kem — without a guard! — on business connected with the commandant's office. He forged all the necessary documents for himself — in an assumed name: a railway pass, even a certificate of membership of the Communist Party. Then he went to Kem, allegedly on business — and never came back. Many weeks later we got a letter saying that Nikolaeff was in Moscow, sent us his kind remembrances, and wished us a speedy departure southward.

Every other attempt to escape had invariably ended in the fugitives being captured and put to a torturing death. It was so with the Finlander who tried to escape in March, 1925, and with Captain Skhyrtladze's party. Six "K.R.'s," headed by Captain Skhyrtladze, escaped from the Solovetsky Monastery in a boat which they had got hold of after killing a sentry. For five days they were tossed about in a rough sea, trying to make the shore near Kem. They had no food, their strength gave out, and several times the idea of committing suicide by upsetting the boat presented itself to them. At last one of the unhappy Columbuses cried "Land!" They came to the shore and landed at night. They were so weak and exhausted that, having lit a fire in the woods, they forgot everything else and fell down beside it half dead. A patrol from the Solovky found them there. The Tchekists flung bombs at the fire. Four of the fugitives were killed on the spot; the two others, one of whom was Captain Skhyrtladze, were recaptured. Skhyrtladze had one hand blown off and both legs broken. They were taken to hospital, given some treatment, and then, after cruel tortures, were shot.

Only a miracle, a direct act of God, could make the impossible possible. But we — I and my four comrades — believed in miracles, and prayed to God for one. And He led us for thirty-five days through the marshes of Karelia and the forests of the border region, and on the thirty-sixth day brought us to Kuusamo, in Finland.

II. LAYING OUR PLANS

Cautious Reconnaissance Work — Bezsonoff's Arrival — Our Party Made Up — Elaborate Contrivance Necessary — A Critical Moment.

The thought of escape was always in my mind, even in the Caucasus, in the prisons of the Extraordinary Commissions of Batoum, Tiflis, Vladikavkaz and Grozny. On my arrival in the Solovky, I first began to sound the possibilities in this direction. In the concentration camps of the north, inquiries of this kind have to be made with extreme caution; the greatest delicacy must be employed in asking questions and reconnoitring the ground. You cannot tell which of the prisoners are secret agents of the Gpu and which are people who feel as you yourself do. There have been many cases in which educated prisoners, at first sight most charming fellows, have betrayed their companions.

In the winter of 1924-25 I became intimate with the medical student Nikolaeff. He told me that he was making preparations to escape. We did not agree, however, as to what should be done in the next stage. Nikolaeff insisted that we should escape into the interior of Russia, with correct papers, which he promised to forge. As described in the last chapter, he did this successfully on his own behalf. I, on the contrary, was for escaping abroad, for two reasons, viz.: (1) even if we succeeded in escaping, the Tchekists would probably find us very soon if we stayed in Russia; (2) my destination, the Caucasus, was too distant from the Solovky for me to be sure of getting there. So, while Nikolaeff succeeded in making his escape to Moscow via Kem and Petrograd, I stayed in the Solovky to wait for a more favourable opportunity.

One Saturday in February, 1925, a new convoy of "K.R.'s" arrived in the Solovky. Among the prisoners was a former captain in the Life Guards Dragoon Regiment named Bezsonoff. He had not been two days in the camp before he asked me:

"What do you think about escaping? I mean to clear off from here pretty soon."

As I had every reason to believe that I was dealing with a Gpu spy, I replied:

"I don't mean to try to escape. I'm all right here."

But soon I got to know Bezsonoff better. He had been transported to

Tobolsk for "counter-revolution" and repeated attempts to escape from captivity. He managed to escape from Tobolsk and got to Petrograd, where he lived in freedom for six months. Then he again fell into the hands of the Gpu, which sentenced him to be shot, but his sentence was commuted to five years in the Solovky, to be followed by a period of exile in the Narym region. In the camp he bore himself with an independent air, openly abused the Tchekists, and did not obey the orders of the personnel.

We decided to escape into Finland. Each of us sought for companions in the adventure among our fellow-prisoners. Bezsonoff came to an understanding with two Poles named Malbrodsky and Sazonoff. Malbrodsky was a particularly valuable comrade because he had a compass. While in the Tcheka prison at Minsk, he had hidden his compass in a cake of soap, and had brought it, thus concealed, to the Solovky. Of course we had no maps of any kind. Our marching orders were simply — westward! Here the compass would play a decisive part.

Only prisoners engaged in outside labour had a chance of flight. Of late I had had the duty of making out the lists of prisoners detailed for various kinds of work outside the camp. I myself, however, was not allowed by the Tchekists to go outside the wire fence, as they had suspected me for a long time past of intending to make a bolt. I was faced with the difficult task of making out a list of workers consisting only of men useful to us, and getting my own name on to the list in addition.

As a rule, parties from five to twelve strong are detailed for work outside the camp. Too large a party was no use to us. It was indispensable that a party of five should be made up consisting of the four already mentioned — Bezsonoff, Malbrodsky, Sazonoff and myself — and a reliable "K.R." I managed to add a Kuban Cossack to the list. He was not warned in advance.

We had still one obstacle to overcome. Each party was, as a rule, composed of prisoners belonging to the same labour company. Bezsonoff belonged to the 5th company, but Sazonoff, for example, to the 7th. Although I was continually in danger of ruining the whole laboriously contrived scheme, I nevertheless managed to get all our men into one party.

Early in the morning of May 18th, 1925, two parties, among others, were taken to work outside the camp. A party from the 6th company was taken to cut wood on the shore near Kem, and another — ours — to clean out the Red soldiers' barracks, on Popoff Island itself. This threatened to ruin the whole plan — it was impossible to get away from Popoff Island.

All this time a Tchekist named Myasnikoff had been keeping a particularly watchful eye on me. He sometimes said he had been a hussar, sometimes a sailor, sometimes a colleague of Dzerzhinsky; in the camp he was deputy-commander of a labour regiment. I had, under his eyes, to invent some reason for sending our party to the woods, and not the other. After a minute's thought, I went up to the party from the 6th company and said:

"You fellows'll be simply frozen in the woods with such rags on, and only bast shoes. You'd better go to the barracks."

Our men had specially mended their clothes and boots for the occasion.

Luckily for us, just at this moment Myasnikoff was called away for some reason or other. I led our party up to the guards, and said:

"Now, comrades, take us off to work in the woods."

Never has my heart beaten as it did in that minute. They gave us an escort of two Red soldiers, and took us off to work.

III. OUR FLIGHT: THE FIRST STAGE

An Initial Success — Covering our Tracks — Bezsonoff as Dictator
— Traces of our Pursuers — A Trap.

We cut wood till 8 a.m. At that hour a goods train came from Popoff
Island to Kem; it would have been dangerous to try to escape before then.
When the train had disappeared, Bezsonoff gave the signal arranged long
before — he turned up his collar. We flung ourselves on the soldiers from
behind. We succeeded in disarming one of them immediately. The other
pushed away Malbrodsky and Sazonoff, whose business it was to disarm
him, and began to yell. Luckily we were nearly three miles from the camp.
I gave the Red soldier a blow in the side, and he fell.

I was for shooting the two soldiers; they were both Communists and
belonged to the Gpu troops. But Bezsonoff persuaded me not to do so,
arguing that an act of vengeance at such a moment was useless, and that
no one would gain anything by it.

At that moment the Kuban Cossack, who had flung himself on the
ground in surprise, stretched out his hands to us, and cried:

"Little brothers, don't kill me!"

We calmed him.

"What are you making all this noise about, you fool? Nobody's going
to kill you. The freedom you had in the Solovky Kalinin gave you, we
give you the freedom you have now. Do as you like. If you go back to the
camp you'll be shot. If you come with us, there's a risk there too. Or, if
you like, go south on your own, to the Kuban. We can do without you.
Do as you like."

The Cossack came with us. His name, by the way, was Pribludin.

We had decided long before to cover our tracks in every possible
way. Our real objective being the frontier between Russia and Finland,
which lay to westward, we went due north for twenty miles along the
railway embankment, taking the two Red soldiers with us. After covering
nine miles, we sent one of the soldiers off in a westerly direction, and the
second when we had gone eleven miles, first taking off their boots. We
reckoned that even if they found the way back they would not reach the
camp before the following morning.

We came to a railwayman's hut. We asked the pointsman to sell us bread (we had six tchervontsy, which we had saved while we were preparing to escape), but the man, apparently a Communist, refused. We had to take the food by force. We loaded up Pribludin, Sazonoff and Malbrodsky with the provisions and went on for three miles in a northerly direction, then turned east, then south, and came back almost to the same place from which we had started northward two days before. We crossed the railway embankment and steered due west.

During these first days we walked without a break, either by day or by, night. The "rests" mentioned in Bezsonoff's diary, which he kept on the inside of the cover of his Bible, were halts of a few minutes only for food. Our weariness soon began to make itself felt. There were no roads; our route lay over damp ground, covered with thick undergrowth, and endless marshes. Bezsonoff, who had constituted himself an inexorable dictator to the rest of us, brandished a rifle under the nose of anyone who stopped even for a minute, and threatened to kill him on the spot. At the time we thought him cruel, but I know now that the merciless insistence of our "dictator" contributed in a high degree to the success of our flight.

We changed direction sharply once again and marched southward, towards the river Kem. A snowstorm overtook us. The violence of the tempest blew us off our legs. My boots got burnt through at a fire; luckily I had an old pair of goloshes with me, and put them on, winding strips of rag round my legs. It is possible that the fearful blizzard, which caused us such hardships, benefited us at the same time, for the snow covered our tracks.

Our bread was all finished. We had thirty bits of sugar left. We had introduced a "starvation ration," and were sharing out every crumb, when we came to the hamlet Poddiujnoe.

ROUGH MAP SHOWING OUR ROUTE
(marked with dots).

1. Solovetsky Island (in reality much farther from the mainland).
2. Rymbaki.
3. Popoff Island.
4. Kem.
5. Poddiujnoe.
6. River Kem.
7. River Shomba.
8. Wooden road.
9. Lake Toro.
10. Lake Muojärvi.
11. Main road from Kuusamo to Uleaborg.

Near the hamlet we found the footmarks of Tchekists. As Bezsonoff had on a pair of Government boots, taken from one of the Red soldiers, we were able to compare the tracks and ascertain that the footmarks were those of soldiers belonging to the Gpu troops. We also found the footmarks of police dogs. So we knew that we were being hunted with dogs.

We decided to go on westward along the bank of the river Kem, without making any detour. My feet were so badly frost-bitten that the pain sometimes brought tears into my eyes, but there was nothing for it but to go on and on. About ten miles from Poddiujnoe we met two Karelians. On seeing us they were filled with horror at our convict-like appearance, and at our situation. They told us that all Karelia had been informed by telephone that five men had escaped from the Solovky, and ten poods of flour promised for each fugitive handed over. They had seen ten Tchekists with dogs. Moreover, a motor launch from Kem, with six men on board, was patrolling the river.

We asked the Karelians for bread and tobacco. They gave us two loaves and a packet of makhorka (coarse tobacco), for which we paid three roubles — they had no change. They advised us to make for a dairy farm twenty miles from Poddiujnoe. We found, in due course, that a regular trap had been laid for us at this dairy farm. But I do not think the two Karelians sent us into it intentionally.

As a rule, when we came near a human habitation, we lay on the ground for two hours, watching to see who went into and came out of the house. We did so this time, and saw nothing suspicious. Sazonoff, Malbrodsky and Pribludin remained behind, while Bezsonoff and I went forward. The house stood apart from the farm buildings. Bezsonoff opened the door. In the very act of entering he gave a wild yell of "Red soldiers!" On opening the door, he saw right in front of him three rifles aimed at him. Being an exceptionally cool-headed man, he did not lose his head, but instantly slammed the door to and fired through it.

I leapt to the door. The Red soldiers kept quite still. It would have been stupid to fight them. We decided to retreat to the woods. But we had to pass the window of the house, and the Tchekists would have shot us down from the window like partridges. Bezsonoff took up a position close to the stables, in a place from which he could fire at the window at any moment if one of the soldiers showed himself at it; I stood on the other side, also holding my rifle at the ready.

Then, abandoning our posts, we gave ourselves the order, "Quick — bolt!" and were about to make for the woods when a motor launch, with six soldiers on board, came up to the bank from the direction of the mouth of the Shomba, a tributary of the Kem. The Red soldiers in the house leapt out of the windows on the opposite side, facing the river. I did not see any use in firing. Bezsonoff, however, fired at the launch. The Tchekists leapt ashore and flung themselves into the woods. Weeping and wailing arose from another boat, loaded with women and children, the families of Karelian fishermen. We retired hastily into the woods.

IV. A TERRIBLE MARCH

Sazonoff as Raft-builder — A Bitter Disappointment — A Hay-maker's Larder — We Pillage a Communist's Farm — A Narrow Shave — Sazonoff's Swimming Achievement.

We recommenced our exhausting journey through the marshes, covered with thick scrub. We had no food. Despair took the place of hope in our hearts. Time after time we fell down from exhaustion and weariness. My frost-bitten feet caused me fearful torment.

We continued to follow the river Kem almost due south, then turned west. Thus, falling and getting up, and falling into the water again, we covered twenty-five miles. We came to a big lake, with fishermen's huts on the shore. The men were not at home. We took a quantity of food and left a tchervonets on a stone with a note which ran:

"We are sorry, but necessity compels us to steal. We leave you a tchervonets."

For a long time we did not know how to get across the lake. We tried to go round, and walked ten miles — still we were confronted by water. Then Sazonoff, who had grown up in the neighbourhood of water, made some odd little rafts, fastening planks together with everything we had — rifle slings, belts, shirts — and brought us over to the other side. This voyage across the lake, I remember, used up what little energy we still had. Indeed, when I now recall all that we went through in those dreadful days, I cannot understand how we endured such a strain, both physical and mental, and how it was that we did not fall down dead somewhere in the Karelian mosses. But evidently God thought fit to save us, to bring us out of the dense, marshy jungle, that we might bear witness to the whole world of the place of torment into which a loathsome government has turned the once holy Solovetsky Monastery.

After crossing the lake, we decided to march due west. More marshes in endless succession, no paths, not a scrap of bread. We usually endured the pangs of hunger for three days, and on the fourth day went in search of bread, at the risk of falling into a trap. While in search of provisions, we came upon a wooden road through the marshes, evidently laid down by the British. We could see no tracks on it. We held a council of war, and decided to turn off northward in the hope of coming to a habitation. We covered twenty miles: not a soul.

Then we came to another lake, and there, on the other side, was a large village. We could hear voices and the barking of dogs. We dragged ourselves to the bank. Bezsonoff and Sazonoff stood by the water's edge for a long time, and shouted:

"Hallo! Hallo!"

At last we made ourselves heard. A boat came over, rowed by a Karelian.

"Can we get any bread? We'll pay for it."

"Yes, you can get bread, you can get anything you like," the honest fisherman replied. "But there are Tchekists from the Solovky in the village, searching for you."

Once more we had to plunge into the depths of the scrub. It rained unceasingly, the days were raw and windy. For four more days we had nothing to eat. We had only our tobacco.

At last we came to a wooden footpath raised above the water. We went along it and came to a tiny hut in the middle of the marshes. We examined the little place carefully, but could find nothing eatable. While the rest of us were making a fire of brushwood in the rain, Bezsonoff continued to prospect in the neighbourhood of the hut, and suddenly returned from his reconnaissance with five loaves of black bread in his hands. He ate greedily as he walked. I thought at first it was a hallucination caused by hunger, but no, it was real bread, and plenty of it!

It was evidently a hut belonging to Karelian hay-makers. They bring their stores of food to their huts in winter, because in summer it is impossible to get to them; the marshes are turned into an inland sea. Not far from our hut Bezsonoff found a wooden shelter like a gigantic mushroom, with an opening in the middle, and under it exactly a hundred huge loaves, three bags of groats and a bag of salt. Our joy knew no bounds. We decided to have a good rest. Happily, the possibility of a Tchekist ambush in the midst of the marshes — the passage of which was quite impracticable except by a footpath such as we had found — could be almost entirely dismissed. We made out of that bread (in fancy) tea, cooked meat and various kinds of soup! We lived in the hut until each of us had five cakes of bread left.

Then — westward once again! Water, water, water without end. We marched for nearly a week on the five cakes per man. We found a path, which led us to a lonely dairy farm. We hid, kept our ears open, and finally sent Sazonoff on to get food. When he came back with bread and butter we noticed that a peasant woman ran out of the cottage and hurried to a boat which lay by the bank. We had evidently come to a Communist's house, and the woman had gone to fetch Red soldiers. We fired a few shots after her; she took fright and went back to the house.

We pillaged those Communists without mercy. We took a tub of butter, a lot of white bread, and all the fish there was in the house. We had now so much food that even Bezsonoff and I, who usually walked at the head of the party in "light marching order," rifle in hand, had each of us to shoulder a sack.

We were by this time simply in rags. The thorny bushes had torn our clothes to shreds; our boots had come unstitched. With tangled beards, incredibly filthy faces, holes at knees and elbows, we looked like cannibals, or escaped convicts — which, for that matter, was just what we were.

Going along a narrow path through the woods, we came upon tracks of Red soldiers' boots and the stump of a makhorka cigarette. As we had no tobacco left by then, we eagerly seized the stump, and each of us had two puffs at it. Sazonoff and Malbrodsky insisted that we should leave the dangerous path. We came to a river. We looked for a ford for over three hours, but could not find one, and had to go back to the path we had abandoned.

After we had walked for a long time we came to a place where the marks of many feet were plainly visible. We knew from this that we were quite close to the frontier; but we could not say even approximately where the frontier was. We had no map, and none of us knew how many miles we had to go to reach Finland. The arrow of the compass showed us where west lay, and that was all.

We followed the tracks cautiously. We had just gone round a slight hillock, when from behind a big rock there came a hail of bullets. I was so taken by surprise that I stopped dead. Fifty or sixty rounds were fired at us point blank. We saw the flashes from the rock. But not one of us was touched. Not till then did we perceive that the ambush was laid on both sides of the path. The woods, particularly dense at that spot, saved us. We scattered among the undergrowth. The firing went on for a long time. It may have been the Soviet frontier patrol we had encountered.

Moving swiftly westward, we came to a halt again at the river. We could still find no ford. We tried to find a way round; we went a long way and came back again. We learnt a few days later that this stream was the frontier between Russia and Finland. It is considered impassable, and is, therefore, guarded by neither Finlanders nor Russians.

But cross the river we must; it blocked our route westward. Sazonoff swam to the opposite bank. Malbrodsky plunged into the water and began to drown. The strong current swept him downstream; I dragged him out with difficulty. I myself was carried for several yards downstream; I began to suffocate, but in the nick of time I stuck the muzzle of my rifle into the river bottom and supported myself on it. We did not know what to do. We had no strength at all. We jumped recklessly into the water several times, and every time returned to the bank completely exhausted. Then Sazonoff gave us another exhibition of his skill in mastering any current; he carried each of us in turn over to the opposite bank on his back!

This was at three o'clock on the morning of June 15th.

V. FREEDOM

Linguistic Difficulties — Joyful Certainty — Bezsonoff's Diary —
Finnish Peasant's Claim for Damages — A Friend in Need — Free at Last.

We had not a dry thread on us. Our cartridges were soaked. Our
fingers shook with cold, we could not speak to one another. To crown
all, our small supply of bread had run out. Luckily, a couple of days later
we came upon a deer in the woods, and Bezsonoff, who had contrived,
unlike the rest of us, to keep his ammunition dry, shot it. In our joy we
ate half of it at once without bread. We made soup out of a part of it, and
took the cooked meat that was left over along with us. The result of this
feast was that we all fell ill with an acute gastric disorder, and for several
days were so weak that we could hardly walk.

After a long tramp we came, two days after we had crossed the river,
to a cottage. We went in and asked the people to sell us bread and other
food. They could not speak or understand a word of Russian. Supposing
ourselves to be already in Finland,[35] we repeatedly asked:

"Where are we? What is this? Finland? Russians?"

We had recourse to mimicry, to talking on our fingers. It was quite
useless. (On arriving in Finland, by the way, we discovered that the Finnish name for the country is Suomi.)

We took some food of various kinds, and offered them a tchervonets.
They would not take it. We gave them all our small change, ninety silver
kopeks; they took the silver. We went off, followed by unfriendly looks.

Several more days passed, full of uncertainty. Had we crossed the
frontier or not? Were we in Finland or still in the U.S.S.R.? If we assumed
the former to be the case, did we not risk making our escape a failure
after all the difficulties we had overcome, and falling into the hands of
the Tchekists again?

On June 23rd we came to a big river. There were a crowd of people
on the opposite bank; evidently wood-floating was in preparation. We
had noticed during the past week a certain change in our surroundings,
signs of order and culture; and we had found a cigarette box with an
inscription that was not in Russian. The workmen on the river bank were

35   Language was not a certain guide, as the peasants on both sides of
the frontier are Finnish-speaking.

107

much better clothed than Russian workmen are. After long hesitation and uneasiness we decided that the frontier lay behind us. We called for a boat to be sent from the other side. The workmen who came across explained to us, certainly not without difficulty, that the U.S.S.R. lay far in our rear.

For a moment or two we could not utter a word for mingled joy and weariness; all our strength seemed suddenly to leave us. Bezsonoff chronicled that unforgettable moment in his diary in one significant word: "Finland."

Our "dictator" kept this diary on the inside of the cover, the back of the table of contents, and the last (440th) page of the "New Testament of Our Lord Jesus Christ" (Synod edition of 1916). He made short pencil notes daily. These disconnected entries, which had in truth been through fire and water, give the clearest possible picture of all the vicissitudes of our flight. It was thanks to them that we did not lose count of the days.

I give some typical extracts from Bezsonoff's diary:

May   18th, 1925. — Disarmed escort and escaped. . . . .
"   21st. — Bivouac in woods. Stayed in hut on
account of snowstorm. . . . .
"   24th. — Snow continued. Stopped in evening. . . .
"   26th. — Snow thawing. At 2 p.m. started for
river Kem, at 7 p.m. came to hamlet
Poddiujnoe. 11 p.m., met two peasants.
Got some bread. Night. Going along
river Kem. In good spirits. At
Poddiujnoe ambushes of Red soldiers, who
went off in search of us.
May   27th. — Marched all night and day without rest.
Food quite finished. At 7 p.m. came to
dairy farm 22 miles from Poddiujnoe.
Going into farm fell into ambush of Red
soldiers. After firing Red soldiers cleared
off in boat. We hurried along Kem,
getting food from fishermen. Not much
food. Have to go hungry. Horribly
tired. At 2 a.m. left bank of Kem and
halted for rest at 6 a.m.
"   28th. — Rested all day. Little to eat. All have
legs badly swollen. . . . .
"   29th. — Night march through "impassable"
marshes. Day resting. Pushed on in

evening. Rest. Cloudberries, geese, hare.
Midnight. Malbrodsky unable to march
from exhaustion, rested. . . .
"   30th. — About 11 p.m. successfully crossed r.
Shomba. Relief and joy great. God be
praised. Marched all night. . . . .
June   1st. — In the morning unexpectedly came to
fishermen's hut; they were out fishing.
Took bread from them, leaving 3 roub.
Great help. Going on. Lost our way
among lakes. Made raft. Ferried over.
Creator. Nearly morning. All slept.
God be praised. Help us in the future
also, O God, and save us from our enemies.
And I believe He will help us.
June   6th. — Rest. The little hut. At the moment I
am morally and physically a happy man.
Nature, sky, beauty. . . . God has wrought
a miracle.
"   8th. — Weather changed. Warm. Water falling.
Eat every 2 hours and thank God. Almost
night. Fire. I cannot sleep. I keep watch.
Situation good. Nothing of note. We
reckon we have covered 18 miles of
"impassable" marshes. . . .
"   11th. — Marched all night. In the morning stopped
for "short halt" to drink hot water.
Went on. Rested at 6 p.m. Little hut
No. 2. Moved on in evening. So much
the nearer our goal. I reckon we are
thirteen miles from frontier. I have two
pieces of bread left, Malbrodsky none at all.
"   12th. — Early this morning drank hot water in little
shed by lake. Paths, lake, rain. Halt in
broken-down hut. Nervy. No food.
Lord help us! Went on in evening.
Marching all night. Rain. Dew. Cold.
Path.
June   13th. — Lake. Red soldiers. Line of patrols? Go
round. Rest without fire. Nearly 6 miles
west and no sign of frontier. According to
my reckoning we crossed the frontier at
12 p.m. Marched all night. Cold. Lit
fire and halted till morning. No food at

all.
"   14th. — River. Retreat. Path. Ambushes. Shots
point blank. God saved us. Praise Him.
Flight. Back to river. Ghastly crossing.
"   15th. — Rest after crossing. Spent day and night
drying ourselves. Shared out food. Quarrel.
Peace made. . . .
"   17th. — Killed deer by lucky shot. . . . Ate nearly
all.
"   18th. — Moved off in morning. Halted for rest at
12 p.m. Stopped all day.
"   19th. — At 7 p.m. crossed a clearing. Rested.
Clearing leads nowhere. Raid on dairy
farm. Rest "with cows." . . . .
"   21st. — Moved off in morning. Exhaustion.
Uncertainty. Reluctance to march.
Clearing. Came to an end. Came out on
clearing. Telephone line. River. Wood-
floating. Finland!
Bezsonoff evidently did not note all the days in his diary, for in reality
our flight came to an end on June 23rd, 1925.

The Finlanders received us very kindly, gave us food in abundance
and sent us to Uleaborg. The Chief of Police of Uleaborg moved us all
to tears by his attentions; he not only brought a quantity of food to the
prison for us, and supplied us with money, but he took me himself to a
doctor to have my frost-bitten feet bound up. I, in outward appearance a
complete bandit, dirty and in rags, felt strange in his smart carriage, and
could read on the faces of the people we met the dubious query: "Who
on earth is that convict in the Chief of Police's trap?"

We were, however, not liberated immediately. It appeared that the
owner of the dairy farm from which we had taken food a few days before,
paying for it with only about a rouble in silver (as the people would not
take our Soviet paper money), had made a complaint against us, demanding compensation to the amount of 1,000 marks. The newspapers, pri-
vately informed of the occurrence, wrote that "five Bolshevist bandits had
crossed the frontier and made an armed raid on a Finnish dairy farm."
While this affair was being settled, we had to spend several weeks in
prison, first at Uleaborg and then at Helsingfors. But even prison seemed
paradise to us after the Solovky and the Karelian jungles!

When we arrived at Helsingfors, the president of the special committee for Russian affairs in Finland, A. N. Fenoult, came to see us in prison.

Thanks to his extraordinary energy, and the infinite trouble he took on our behalf, we were very soon set at liberty, and were able to get ourselves decent clothes and assume once more a human aspect. It was significant that Malbrodsky (the other Pole, Sazonoff, being a native of the former Government of Vilna, was not recognised as being a Polish subject), who had immediately appealed to the Polish Consul, did not leave prison until later than we, who had no official diplomatic protection.

I should like to conclude my simple narrative by expressing our heartfelt gratitude to all, both Finlanders and Russians, from whom, on our arrival in Finland, we received so much kindness and sympathy. After the ferocity shown by man towards man in the concentration camps, after the devastating egoism, the hardness, the inhuman callousness, with which the Bolsheviks have inoculated the unhappy Russian people, the reception we met with in Finland touched us to the bottom of our hearts.

A "Mother of the Gulag"

The Solovki Special Camp (later the Solovki Special Prison) was established in 1923 on the Solovetsky Islands in the White Sea as a distant and inaccessible confinement facility for socialist opponents of Soviet Russia's new Bolshevik authority.

Anarchists, Mensheviks, and Socialist Revolutionaries were first exempt from work. The guards and regular criminals worked together to keep the "politicals" in order as priests, nobility, and White Army commanders joined them.

The Gulag evolved from this location because it was near the Five-Year Plans' first major building project, the White Sea-Baltic Canal.

Solovki and the White Sea Canal violated a Gulag regulation by being too near to the border. This allowed many daring escapes in the 1920s and closed the Solovki special jail in the late 1930s due to war. The authorities either shot or transported many thousand convicts on the mainland and Solovki.

MONASTERY TO CONCENTRATION CAMP

The Solovetsky Islands housed the Russian Orthodox Solovetsky Monastery. It was an industrial hub with over 300 monks and a northern Russian naval forepost that repelled foreign invasions throughout the Time of Troubles, Crimean War, and Russian Civil War. Monastery to concentration camp conversion started in fall 1922. They burned all the wooden structures and killed numerous monks, including the Igumen. Central Russian forced labor camps received the surviving monks.

The monastery buildings were converted into the Solovki "special" camp, Solovetsky Lager Osobogo Naznachenia (SLON in Russian), by an unreported edict on November 3, 1923. As one of the earliest "forced labor camps," Solovki was a precursor to the Gulag. People sometimes called it Severnye (Solovetskiye) Lagerya OGPU, meaning "Northern (Solovki) camps of OGPU" in 1924.

The monastery's secluded location made escape difficult, and the Tsarist government utilized it as a political jail. After S. A. Malsagoff's book An Island Hell was published in England, Western Europe and the US criticized the Soviet-era camp's treatment of captives. After a thorough clean-up and meticulous staging, the Soviet authorities dispatched proletarian writer Maxim Gorky there to offset this unfavorable press. He lauded the islands' natural beauty in a positive article, although other writers feel he grasped the genuine realities.

THE BALTIC-WHITE SEA CANAL

The number of inmates transferred to Solovki between 1923 and its closing in 1939 is unclear. Tens to hundreds of thousands are estimated.

In 1923, Soloviki housed "no more than 3,000" convicts; by 1930, it held "about 50,000," with an additional 30,000 detained at Kem, the closest railhead. The early 1930s White Sea-Baltic Canal, one of Stalin's ambitious ambitions, employed many camp detainees [citation required].

A SPECIAL PRISON, 1936-1939

The Solovki camp was declared a "special" jail (STON, Russian for "Groan") in 1936 and held numerous detainees who were killed there or on the mainland during the Great Terror of 1937–1938 until its closing in 1939.

Before documentation verifying their execution were uncovered in 1996, it was believed that over 1,000 detainees, a quota for "1st category arrests" (executions), drowned when their barges were purposely sunk in the White Sea. They were shot on the mainland in late October and early November 1937, but later quotas were shot on the islands near Sekirnaya Hill because they were too late to travel across the White Sea.

NKVD Captain and senior executioner Mikhail Matveyev killed all but five of the 1,116 Solovki inmates brought across the White Sea on October 27, 1937, at Sandarmokh between then and November 10, 1937, when he pronounced his mission accomplished. 289 Executed Renaissance Ukrainian intellectuals were slain.

They readied another ship to go to the mainland for execution, but it was too late in the year to traverse the frozen sea. Instead, they shot 200–300 inmates on Solovki near Sekirnaya Hill. Engineer Yelizaveta Katz, eight months pregnant, was one of many casualties. She was permitted to give birth before being shot with the others on February 17, 1938, then three months later on May 16, 1938, at 28.

The jail closed in 1939. It was too near to Finland's border, and WWII was coming. They made it a naval base and stationed cadets. Valentin Pikul, future novelist, was a student.

LEGACY AND WORLD HERITAGE CONTROVERSY

In 1989, the islands' museum opened "The Solovki Special Camp," the first Gulag exhibit in the USSR. The islands had their inaugural Days of Remembrance for Political Repression Victims in June, followed by August festivities.

The Orthodox Church refounded the monastery and inscribed it to UNESCO's World Heritage List in 1992.

Human rights campaigners lamented that officials were "gradually removing all traces of the labor camp." in 2015. In January 2016, new Solovki Museum director Vladimir Shutov and Archimandrite Porfiry closed the Gulag area.

In August 2017, municipal officials requested police investigate the 29th annual Days of Remembrance as a "unauthorized" event. Archimandrite Porfiry unsuccessfully petitioned an Arkhangelsk Region court to break a 2011 contract with the museum's now-disbanded Gulag division director and remove Olga Bochkaryova and her daughter from their two-room apartment in early 2018.

Multiple Solovki author Yury Brodsky was accused of "religious hatred" in his current novel by an Orthodox website.

NOTABLE CONVICTS

Many Solovki captives were intellectuals from Tsarist Russia and the post-revolutionary USSR.

THE 1920S

Many Solovki survivors were liberated in the 1920s but later arrested and imprisoned or deported.

FIRST FIVE-YEAR PLAN, 1928–1932

Solovki prisoner Naftaly Frenkel led the security services during the First Five-Year Plan.

He was imprisoned for 10 years by the OGPU in 1923 and transferred to Solovki. In 1927, they shortened his sentence, pardoned him, and named him SLON's production chief before sending him to Moscow as a camp representative in 1929. He quickly managed Gulag production and White Sea Canal operations. He participated in the Gulag during the Soviet Union's forced industrialization and collectivization of farmland.

The 1929 Solovki mass shooting, reported by Dmitry Sergeyevich Likhachov and featured in Marina Goldovskaya's 1987 film Solovki Power, signaled the regime's harshening.

www.ingramcontent.com/pod-product-compliance
Lightning Source LLC
Chambersburg PA
CBHW070833100426
42813CB00003B/604